Kiki

and the bird whisperer

Marja Healy

Cover image: lineartestpilot/Shutterstock.com
Back cover image: Jeffrey Turner

www.marjahealy.com

ISBN: 1480244902
ISBN-13: 978-1480244900

For Jeff, who loved Kiki too.
And for my dear sweet Jesus for allowing me precious time
with His majestic common little black bird.

All thanks to Deb and Ken Andersen of Plum River Farm Wildlife Rehab. To Faith Volz for finding my beloved Kiki the help he needed. And to Mary Anne Burkhalter—people caregiver par excellence.

"I tell you, that whenever you refused to help one of these least important ones, you refused to help me."

Matthew 25:45
Good News Bible

TABLE OF CONTENTS

(Author's note: To hear the baby bird's secret words, it's best to read each chapter before viewing the corresponding video at www.marjahealy.com.)

INTRODUCTION
AN ORDINARY DAY

May 29, early afternoon.

Hearing my two white doves coo softly from their cage in the living room, all seemed well in the world. Unable to write when it wasn't, I'd just sat down before my laptop with a steaming mug of coffee. Pausing to look out the open window, rays of sunlight streamed in through the screen. Warming my arms, my face, I'd glanced up at the sky. Eyes on a wide scarf of innocent looking clouds there, I had no way of knowing that they'd hid coming calamity. No—the sky wasn't exactly falling.

But things, quite literally, fell from it sometimes.

And how did the news of that accident come to me exactly? It came like all life altering news arrives nowadays. A cell phone had chirped to life somewhere in the house.

Its ring sounding as insistent as a hungry little bird.

I'd turned around in my chair and looked hesitantly out my bedroom doorway. I'd spied my husband, Jeff, standing there. Fumbling to unsuccessfully find said phone in his multi pocketed cargo pants, he'd missed the call.

As I sat transfixed, wondering who'd called, Jeff pressed a few buttons. Accessing his voicemail, he'd stood with the phone pressed absently to his ear. Listening intently to some message or other, he'd said nothing by way of explanation as to what was going on.

As I hate being left in the dark about anything, I'd had enough. "Well?"

A smile faltering at Jeff's lips, he slid the phone away from his cheek. "All under control."

I'd grimaced. That had to be a lie. What in life was ever under control?

A fake smile plastered upon his face, Jeff then made the return phone call. Immediately. "Hi. It's Jeff. You just called?"

Eavesdropping an impossibility, I'd sat waiting for the bone of a clue to be thrown my way. I'd so hoped that some familiar voice was bearing him good news. But as Jeff stood listening quietly to the voice at the other end of the line, the good-natured smile suddenly fell from his face.

And when it had, my heart sank like a stone in my chest.

Something was wrong somewhere in the world after all. This must have been bad news he was hearing. Propelled out of my chair, I'd moved on wobbly legs and met up with Jeff out in the hallway.

My mouth, dry as cotton. "What is it? What's going on? Is something wrong?"

In answer, he put a hand up in the air to halt my questioning.

Like that would work.

Irritated, if this was bad news I had every intention of getting it over with as quickly as possible. Still, I was helpless, standing there waiting in terror. And being silent not an easy feat for me—acid churned in my stomach. Unable to stand the suspense any longer, I'd stamped a foot on the floor—pissed off royal.

"Who the heck is it? Who's on the phone?" Not knowing what was going on making me temporarily insane, Jeff was in big trouble. "Jeff. Jeff? JEFF!"

My husband had only silently mouthed the name of a friend. *Deb.* Then he'd shrugged his shoulders noncommittally. Whatever that meant. Trying to surmise what could be going on here, I just couldn't tell a thing. All I knew was this. The gal on the other end of the line was an extraordinarily hardworking nurse.

Deb and her husband Ken, a retired police sergeant, had a farm full of rescued domestic animals. The gamut there ran from horses to dogs to cats to pigs. Geese to turkeys to chickens.

Ken and Deb also ran a wildlife rehabilitation center too. Having really big hearts when it came to helping things in need, they'd saved many life forms from certain death over the years. Fawns. Birds of prey. Raccoons. Possums. Squirrels.

"A car came?" Jeff had repeated Deb's words with a casual nod.

A car came what? Me standing mute, listening to him, I was ready to explode. I hated feeling helpless. My mind had been forming pictures from what I could gather from the one sided conversation. I could nearly see the car rolling up Deb's long, dusty stone driveway. Nearly see it park there before their vintage white farmhouse. But why? What did the car bring to them?

"And? And?" My heart slamming my ribcage, I was about to have a fatal heart attack. I was sure of it. I'd soon be dead if I was left in the dark about this one minute longer.

Jeff stood scratching his head unaware death was rearing its ugly head somewhere in his near vicinity. "A baby bird? Uh huh."

Adrenaline shot through my veins. I was left unsteady on my feet. These three measly words—stuck in my brain like a hot poker.

A baby bird.

Armed with actual news, I'd listened further. This time without going berserk. It appeared that Deb was about to leave for work. When a caring young woman named Faith had dropped off a baby bird. It also appeared that Ken would not be able to care for the baby bird on this day—various appointments to keep.

Us, all living in the country, having appointments meant they'd be spread out. Far and wide. Ken would be busy all day long, everything here being miles away from anywhere else. Everything here took forever to get to. And forever to get back from. Never ones to refuse a challenge lightly, on this day, Ken and Deb had to. And so then, the words Jeff had uttered now ripped through my heart like a fresh wound.

A baby bird.

Having once been a volunteer at a county wildlife rehabilitation center, I knew the true meaning behind the words *baby bird*. It meant that without immediate—and constant care—the little bird would die.

Depending on its age, if it was a hatchling or a nestling, it would need a feeding every twenty minutes or so. Without such care, a baby bird would not make it to nighttime.

Jeff repeated the conversation again. "It's dehydrated." Silence. "It's not a protected species." Silence. "It has a will to live." Silence. "Can we take it for awhile?"

I stood helplessly watching the wheels in Jeff's head turning.

He was trying to figure out how to say no—without hurting anybody. But it was already too late for that. With Jeff ready to back out, he couldn't. Not with me standing here like a mother hen watching vultures circling her young. The course of my immediate destiny forever altered, my heart was already singing at the prospect of helping.

I furiously nodded my head at Jeff, whispering, "Say yes! Say yes!"

Jeff scowled back at me, shaking his head *no* in response.

With Jeff asking for trouble, I'd stood my ground. Shaking my head *yes* right back at him, the more he shook his head *no*. At an impasse here, it appeared that my high school sweetheart knew me better than I'd known myself. He wasn't about to give in to this *baby bird* thing that easily. He knew I'd upend my life to save an animal in need.

And this was a bird, no less.

A. Baby. Bird.

It would mean many sleepless nights. A huge amount of them. I mean, if the Navy really wanted to train Seal Team Six sleep deprivation, they'd make them feed baby birds around the clock. For weeks on end. Because that's exactly what it takes to make them survive.

But with Jeff adamantly standing his ground, I'd geared up to fight him every step of the way. Sure, I knew what this meant to my life too, caring for a baby bird. Back at the wildlife center, I'd always suffered impossible heartbreak when some little life form in our care would suddenly die unexpectedly.

Even if another baby animal gloriously lived, I'd have a hard time saying goodbye to it at release time. Therefore, the outcome being the same—life or death, it all meant one thing to Jeff.

That in the end, my heart would be irreparably broken.

Yes, Jeff only had the best of intentions for me here. Hadn't he recently seen me pick up yet another beer bottle that somebody had flung into our woods? Sitting straight up on a hillside, I'd lifted it to inspect it. Rain water collecting there, three little mice faces trapped inside peered out at me. All dead, drowned, they'd only gone in for a sip of water. No way to tell the careless boozer how deadly their actions were to innocent wildlife, I'd cried for days.

So sure, Jeff knew how easily I could get hurt. But I was out to win this little conflict. This little war that just broken out between us. About to refuse to take the bird in, Jeff was only out to save me from myself. All right. I'd gotten it. Jeff was out to save me from my ridiculously fragile heart. But it was too late. Duty called.

And duty's name was *baby bird*.

Now on a mission, like all duty, this one wasn't about protecting myself. Duty was about saving a life thrown your way at all costs. All of life—precious beyond what mere words could ever convey, I'd so wanted to help this baby.

Appealing to Jeff's inner cream puff, I'd used tears.

Okay, when tears failed the mission, I'd tried to outgun him. A shaky fist hovering in the air before his face, plus tears, it showed him how I'd meant business. That had to be clear. Jeff would acquiesce on the matter. And soon. Or else—no dinner.

Being a lacto-ovo vegetarian cook, I'd send him packing to the nearest fast food joint. To die a horrible death. Prematurely.

Instead, I'd only whispered in my best Dirty Harry voice. "I'll kill you."

As soon as Jeff had a change of heart and smiled, my heart sang. Listening to the fateful words he'd said next, I was *in*. "Sure Deb. We'd love to take the bird." Then he'd listened intently to Deb as an offer was made to drive the baby over to our house.

But I couldn't have her be late for work over this. A nurse, somebody might die if she wasn't there. Pushing Jeff towards the front door, he'd had no choice but to agree with me.

"Not necessary. I'll come right over to get the bird. No. Not a problem. I was just walking out the door. I swear."

Me shooing him out the door, I'd stood there with it open. Suddenly worried I'd made Jeff hurry, he could get into an accident along the way. "Be careful. Don't speed."

So much for that. Not with the sound of squealing tires ripping out the driveway. Jeff's gas pedal hitting the floor, he'd raced the SUV down the hilly country road. A veritable bird ambulance, something had finally occurred to me about the whole endeavor.

I didn't even know what kind of bird would soon be arriving at my house.

And I didn't care either.

With the demanding world of a new baby suddenly, miraculously, upon me I ran around the empty house in preparation. Going light-speed, I was out to make the perfect home for our newly adopted bundle of feathers.

First off, I'd have to find a makeshift nest for this abandoned mystery bird of unknown origins. How? Well, thank God I knew what to do from my previous training at the county wildlife center.

I'd set a clean cat carrier on the kitchen countertop next to the Kitchen Aid beater. The walls glazed a deep honey-mustard color, I could never be tired with all this sunniness around me. And with all the sunshine gleaming off the pots hanging from the wall, I wouldn't need much sleep. Not much sleep at all.

Rummaging the cabinet shelves, the perfect nest was bound to be around somewhere. Settling on an empty plastic parmesan cheese container I'd washed and saved, I had to laugh. Being even more frugal than my late mother, being cheap had its payoffs. After stuffing the plastic container full of toilet paper, I'd draped a nice clean blanket of Kleenex on top of it all. My hands trembling with newfound resolve—this bird would live. It would live.

Or I'd die trying to make it.

No more than twenty minutes after Jeff barreled down the road, he'd pulled the car back into the garage.

I met up with him at the front door, a warm rush of air blowing in. Handing me Deb's cat carrier, and a care-package baggie of dry cat food, my heart raced. Lifting the carrier eagerly to my face, I peered through the door's chrome mesh.

A tiny ball of pink flesh already sitting in a plastic container there, the baby bird was barely pin feathered. Its pink tail nub, not feathered at all. Tufts of grayish baby down sticking wildly from its temples, its beak looked huge. Its head wobbling on a bald scrawny neck, this was bad news. Bad news indeed.

The bird was a mere nestling. Only about a week and a half out of its egg. And if it fell out of a nest, there could be unseen injuries. Injuries that made me crazy with worry.

Still staring into the carrier, the bird's little gray eyes centered right back on mine. Its beak popping open, an earsplitting shriek ripped through the room.

"Mom?" It was as if the baby instantly knew me—the bird having said as much.

In love just like that—my heart sank to my knees.

"Squeaky?" Calling it that, the name could be no other. Not with a high-pitched baby-squawk like that.

But Squeaky's beak stayed open in alarm. "Hungry! Hungry! Hungry!"

Going a thousand miles an hour like a fireman going down a pole, I set off for the kitchen in answer to the call. "Jeff, it's got to eat. Right now. It has to live. It has to!"

Jeff followed me into the kitchen, ever the bearer of bad news. "But sometimes they don't, Marja. Sometimes they don't live."

Though Jeff's words should have made me hysterical, their importance made me get oddly composed. Yes, I was one of those people that got calm when the plane went down.

First, I'd carefully transferred the baby bird's weightless little body to the clean nest I'd prepared. Then I placed its nest on the countertop. Crushing the cat food with a mortar and pestle, I added dry baby cereal flakes and Pedialyte. Getting it to a perfect thick custard consistency, lunch was ready.

Sucking up the mixture in a ten cc syringe, it was one with the entire plastic end lopped off. Sliding the blunted syringe tip carefully into Squeaky's waiting beak, I'd squeezed the plunger in gently. A tiny amount left deep in the baby's throat, I stood waiting for the correct response.

The bird had swallowed. Hard. "Thanks, Mom."

I'd leaned down to peer into its little face. "How can you be so beautiful?"

Jeff, watching me bond instantly with the bird, he'd recognized that I was already a goner. "Is it a starling. A grackle? A cedar waxwing? It's so—*ugly*."

"Shhh, Jeff!" Jeff, having insulted my baby, he'd also insulted me. "The poor thing. You wouldn't believe what it thought when it first saw your bald head."

Jeff ran a hand over his cleanly shaven skull. "You know that, huh, what the bird's thinking? Come on."

I'd nodded I'd indeed known, whispering the secret into Jeff's ear. "The bird. It thought it got abducted by aliens."

Jeff might have laughed it all off, yeah. But I knew he'd eventually horn in on all our private moments together with a video camera on. While film may seem concise, it can't convey what love *feels* like. Or tell a bird's hidden secrets. Or convey his side of the story. So all this, I'd have to put into words. For Kiki's sake. For my own as well. Kiki would be cute on film, yes. Adorable. But there's always more to the story than what's taking place before one's eyes.

For sometimes remembrance is best left to the heart.

CHAPTER 1 (VIDEO 1)
YET ANOTHER FEEDING

June 2, afternoon

Our lives together had started simply enough, Kiki's and mine.
Simple if terror interspersed with dread can ever be simple.
Concerned only with making this baby bird live, Jeff didn't film us
yet either. Taking just one photo of Kiki so far, I was worried the
flash might scare it. Injure its eyes. Whatever.

The worry was mounting. There were some mornings I thought
Kiki wouldn't make it at all. Unable to lift its head. Looking a little
jaundiced. Sick. But regardless, today I'd thought I should at least
try to take another photo.

I could lose this precious little life form at any second, after all.

I found myself standing, tired and unsteady on my feet in the
kitchen. The room's sunny walls and shiny pots doing nothing to
rouse me, how could morning be so long gone? I really should've
been more awake by now. But I wasn't. And no amount of coffee
would do the trick either.

This being the fourth day of feeding the baby bird around the
clock, I now knew what a zombie must feel like. On a bad day, no
less. Catching only a few zzzs here and there, bags hung on the bags
beneath my eyes. My heart slammed my ribcage like an angry fist. I
was dizzy on my feet. Nauseous. Sure I was suffering a heart attack,
I'd resembled the walking dead. Then Jeff went and inadvertently
made me feel worse.

19

Marja Healy

Waltzing into the kitchen with his video camera on, this then would be our first video together—Kiki's and mine.

At first, I had this compunction to act alert. But pretending to be coherent, and really being coherent, are two vastly different things. About to find that fact out the hard way, my sleepy mind wasn't about to cooperate. Unused to sleep deprivation, I'd turned into a tongue tied buffoon of my former sparkling self.

And forgot the bird's name.

I'd wanted to introduce my precious nestling by what I'd previously named him. But having been caught off guard like this—Jeff's camera rolling—I couldn't even remember what that had been. And how? How could I not remember my beloved baby bird's name? The harder I'd tried to remember, the harder my racked brain fought my best intentions.

Did I think to look on the nest, where I'd written the name? Nope.

It had been something that started with the letter S. That was all I could think. I'd remembered having truncated the bird's name down to something easier to say last night. Consonants having become tongue twisters somewhere in the wee hours—that's exactly what happened.

But what had I shortened it down to—and from what—the bird's name?

I'd shortened the moniker down to something easier to say, that's all I knew for sure. Still, I couldn't even remember what I'd been calling the baby up to that point. It. He. She. Still unaware of its gender, I'd simply have to interchange them all until I'd found out for sure about that too.

With my new baby squawking loudly from its plastic nest, I got even more flustered. Hungry, it wasn't about to stop yelling until I'd fed it. Jeff, filming the bird from outside the cat carrier's door, it looked out at us noisily. Insistently.

"Mom. Need food. Hurry up."

I'd stared in through the door's bars at my heart of hearts. The baby was so cute now, some more of its pin feathers having opened. And when its beak popped opened, it was the luscious color of ripe raspberries inside.

My beautiful baby.

Ol' what's his name.

Wanting to take the time to properly introduce him, or her, to the world—my sleepless mind drew a complete blank. I'd merely stammered on, hoping the name would come to me eventually.

"This is um. This is, hmm—the mystery bird. I was calling it, um, what *was* I calling it?" Needing help, I'd finally looked over at Jeff for advice.

"Squeaky."

Mental head slap. Squeaky. Of course. Of course that had been what I'd named it—the bird having squeaked loudly when I'd first met it. And since. Just like it was squeaking now. Mentally challenged like I was, I tried to explain the name change. Thusly, this is how I'd stumbled into our first film together, me and Kiki's.

"So I'm calling it Squeaky. But at two thirty in the morning, it was hard to say the SQ. So I just named it Kiki." Looking down at the bird I'd started to gush in baby talk. "Kiki? Hi Kiki. Hi." I was so impossibly in love already, what was a little lost sleep? I'd do just about anything to make Kiki live.

Those gray, baby bird eyes fastening onto mine inquisitively, Kiki had questions of his own. "Where am I from again?"

I looked at the bird in wonder. "Kiki's from a wildlife center. And I'm raising it for a lady named Deb Andersen."

A really nice lady, I'd hesitated here. Not really knowing if I'd done the right thing, having said Deb's whole name. What if she didn't want it committed to film? I'd change the subject, my heart swelling at seeing the bird.

"Hi Kiki!"

Kiki was a bundle of big ideas in a tiny gray package of fluff. "I'm an eagle, right?"

He'd gotten this idea from seeing the T shirt I was wearing. An American flag on it, I'd explained earlier that the ol' red, white and blue represented the land where he'd lived. That eagles were symbols of freedom. Of patriotism. Of all that America could be.

Mentally cringing for this puny little heartbreaker, Kiki was no eagle.

But since a person should never break a young bird's will with the truth, I'd diverted my attention momentarily to Jeff. "We don't know what it is yet. I think it may be a catbird? Catbird." I repeat the word for the bird's sake. As in hint, hint—I'll love you, eagle or no eagle. "Kiki, Kiki. You're my Kik. Hi Kiki." Having fed Kiki with my syringe, I can see we've captured an awkward moment on film. "Oops."

A baby without embarrassment, the bird remained calm. "Doodle happens."

Grabbing a tissue to clean the nest with, he'd then picked up on my concern. "Let me get this out."

"Mom?" The reddish parts of his non-feathered skin having blushed deeper, I'd just accidentally taught him shame. "Change the subject?"

I do, trying to gloss over the accident for his sake. "Hi Kiki." He's so cute just sitting there, I can barely believe my eyes. "Kik's living in a Tupperware nest."

Yes, the baby had outgrown its little cheese container—already! Yet, this new nest seeming a little too big, I'd taped cardboard to its floor. I couldn't let his legs splay-out when he'd shimmied around in it. Splayed legs being a thing that could cripple a baby bird forever.

And I'd sighed, worried too there could be other problems. Unknown ones. Fractures to its wings from a possible fall. A head injury. Its pin feathers now opening, they could be hiding a cat bite going necrotic.

"I'm fine." The beady little eyes having found mine, Kiki had slaked my heartache. "I'm just hungry. All the time."

The bird's age smack in the gray area between being a helpless nestling and becoming a gawky fledgy, I'd gotten worried. Worried well meaning people might take birds out of a nest to raise themselves. Or perhaps stealing a fledgy waiting on the ground for its parents to feed it. Both scenarios, a likely death sentence to a baby bird.

Unless, of course, that person studied with a licensed rehabber, or wildlife center, beforehand.

"Don't try this at home. Don't try this at home." Sounding harsh, I instead tried to show how messy this endeavor can get. "When you put it in this way," the food, "it comes out the other way. So you have to get ready." For a possible blow out.

Tissue in hand, I feed the bird—then stand at the ready. I wait for Kiki to raise up his backside in order to clear the nest's edge. This instinct being the exact one that helps keep the nest clean out in nature. But Kiki can't do it. Can't clear the side of the fake nest at all because it's too tall. His tail nub nowhere near being able to clear it, that's where I'd come in.

Still, Kiki out to compensate, he dropped down. "I can't do it." His weak legs were unable to hold him up. He'd scooted backwards towards the plastic wall again for another try. Wiggling his tail, negligible pin feathers there, he'd geared up to give it all he'd had.

I stood ready and waiting. "Oop. Here we go. Here we go." But I still had to fumble, nearly missing a grasp on the payload. "Whoa. Whoa. Got it! Success. Success."

Having narrowly caught the doodle with a square of toilet paper, high praise was in order for the baby bird. For just being healthy. For having tried to do the right thing. For just being its wonderfully smart self.

"There's my Kik. There's my Kik. Here you go Kik, here you go. I'm going to give her a worm. A meal worm." I'm back to calling *him* a *her*.

Grabbing the worm with a tweezers, its sharp tip ground off so as to not injure the bird's beak, I dropped the worm. Finding freedom, it wiggled away. It tried to hide itself. It escaped.

Kiki looked my face over as if seeing it for the first time. "Where's your beak? Did it break off? You have no beak."

I concerned myself only with the escapee worm. "Whoop. Where'd it go?" The worm, having dove under all the paper in the nest in effort to save itself, I felt horrible for it. Asking the Lord to bring it to heaven, I'd picked it up again. And plowed forward.

Kiki looked up at the worm, waiting impatiently.

"Here it is. Here you go, Kik." Placing the worm in the bird's mouth, he unfortunately didn't swallow. "Oh, it's coming back out!"

Now I felt doubly bad for the worm, seeing as how it tried to save its own life twice now. Grabbing the syringe, I had to think fast. If I gave the bird a dollop of food as well, he just might swallow both.

"You got to get something in her," I told Jeff while the worm came right back out again. Food or no food, the worm wouldn't go down. But the bird must get insects, needing calcium. "Wait, we have to try this again."

"Mom, you have no beak to use." The baby eyed me as if noticing my incompetence. "Does this mean you're not my real mother?"

I'd chided it softly. "Nobody said I was professional. I'm not a professional mother bird."

And I'd stood there wondering myself. How in the heck did a mother bird get a worm to stay in a baby's mouth? They must pre-kill them or something. Then trying it again—Kiki giving it his all for my sake—I'm stunned it works this time around.

"Kik, there you go, Kik. There you go." With Kiki's help, I now feel better about myself.

And he even forgives me my incompetence. "Thanks—*Mom*."

My chest puffing up with pride, I show the little plastic cup full of food to Jeff in explanation. "This is the other stuff he eats. It's a mixture of cat food, Pedialyte, and baby flakes cereal. There you go."

When Kiki eats again, feeling better for it, I have second thoughts. Having told people what to feed a baby bird, what if they indeed try this at home? And something does go wrong for them? It'll be all my fault.

Kiki sat unaware of my concerns, looking up at me gratefully.

And then I find myself thinking that people should know how to do this in case of an emergency.

"If you want to do this though, you better train at a wildlife center first." Like I had. "Because you'll hurt this animal. You could pierce its little mouth or do it wrong."

Truly, a well meaning person actually could hurt a bird's crop by feeding it the wrong way. A crop injury that would then cause it to die by slow starvation.

Kiki nearly nods in agreement, happy somebody's supplying food. "It's good."

"I know, I know." I praise the little bird way too much, repeating myself like an idiot. "There's my Kik. There's my Kik. Kiki. Kik? Kik? Kik?"

I'd so wanted the bird to remember the name I'd given it. So when it got released into the wild, it would hear my voice saying it. And maybe come back to visit me. Me, the adoptive mother who got left behind.

Kiki had only turned his back on me. "I'm Kiki. I'll remember."

I laugh though secretly worried I'm getting the cold wing. "I'm over here, Kik. Kiki?" I'd turned the nest around, forcing Kiki to face me again. "Hi Kiki. Come on, my sweet pea. What are you doing? What are you doing? You got plans for today?"

Stuck in a plastic nest, nowhere to go, he eyes me. "What do you think?"

The bird sounds far more rational than I do at this point. "What are you going to do? What are you going to do all day? What? What are you going to do? Are you going to beg for food? Yes, food. We love food. Food. I love food." I get all rah, rah about it. "Go, go Kik. Good Kiki. Good Kiki." Leaning my face down into the plastic nest, we'd kissed.

"I love you too."

"I know. I know." But I secretly wonder if Kiki only likes me because I'm the bearer of worms. So caught up in being unsure, not paying attention, the nest gets soiled yet again.

Kiki didn't mean to do. "Sorry."

Grabbing the emergency nest, the one I'd put on top of the carrier, it's already full of clean paper. "We're going to move her into a fresh bed." I carefully pick up bird and place it inside on all the soft, fresh paper. "There. You got it now?" That I'd love you no matter what. "There. Now she's in a clean bed. Right, Kiki? Kik?"

Having been fed, the baby can only nod. Getting sleepy, it ignores my best efforts to perk it up by repeating its name a million times over. But a syringe full of food does the trick. My heart bursting in joy, some abandoned babies are too sick to accomplish eating.

"Good baby. Good baby. Good baby. Yes, you are. Yes you are. Who's the good baby? Kik is. Kik's the good baby."

"And you're the good mother."

In love, I'd tried to explain again what had happened to this baby. How it came to be in my care. "When Kik arrived about four days ago, it barely had any feathers. Kik barely had any feathers." And now it had. "So she's getting bigger every day. Right? Yes. You're my good baby."

Kiki placates all my good intentions by squeaking like a baby bird.

"You're my good baby."

"And you're my good mother."

"I know. I know. Who's the good baby? Kiki is. Kiki! Kiki!"

"I love you." Babies are such perfect creatures.

"I know. I know, I love you. Okay. Let's see. You want another worm?"

"A worm again?" The bird suddenly looked worried, having to fight a worm again.

"You want another worm?" I looked my new baby over, delighted at how cute it is. "I like the fuzz on its head."

"I like the fuzz on your head too." Actually a rude thing to say, the baby could've never known this.

"Yes, I know, sweetheart. I know." I watched Kiki's eyes close. "Oh, now he's tired. Now we're getting sleepy. Now we're getting sleepy. Yes we are."

Thrilled when Kiki had done the least little thing, that's love. Touching the bird, I'd tried to make up for how it must miss the close quarters of its nest mates. Of sleeping pressed up against other little wings or beneath its mother's. Caressing its little body with my hand, the bird had pushed back, loving being touched. Picking up on this, how lonely it must be, I wish again that it could've stayed back in its real nest. With its real mother. And I could just die at how inept I must seem at this.

"You're my Kik. You're my Kik. Yes you are. Yes you are."

The bird looked up at me, misplaced love in its little lost eyes.

"Are you my Kik? Are you my Kik? Do you doubt me?"

Finally, out comes one tired little thought. "I'm your Kiki."

"Yes, Kik. That's my Kik. You're my Kik. There's my Kik. Kik's a baby. Kik's a baby. Yes, Kik's a baby. Kik's a baby. Kik's a baby. Kik's a baby. Kik's a baby. Baby? What? What?"

What is wrong with me?

"Shhh. Sleepy."

I praise on, aware I'm a babbling fool but unable to stop myself. "Kik's a baby." I'd kept saying this, unstoppable in my praise. "Yes you are. Kik's a baby."

"I'm a baby." The tiny lids over the gray irises had fluttered again. "How did I get here again?"

"We don't know what happened. Kik fell out of a nest and was brought into a wildlife center."

His thoughts are sleepy too. "Am I an eagle? Am I?"

His hopes breaking my heart, I won't exactly say no. "The mystery bird. Right, Kik? What are you going to do today? You got plans?"

The question was boring to Kiki. "Just, sleepy."

"Tired? Tired? Yeah. Kik's tired. Now what do you want to do? Sleep? You want to go to sleep? Hmm? Come on. Let's eat some more, Kik."

"I couldn't eat another beakful."

I try to rouse him—her—with the tip of the syringe. Out to get in another feeding to buy myself some time later on. "Kik? Kiki! Tired?"

"No more food." The beak remains closed. "Tired."

"Aw. All right. That's all right. We could do this later." I'd then felt guilty I'd tried to force it to eat. "We could do this later. We could. Want to? You want to do this later? Kiki?"

"Shhh."

I'd made my plans to see him in about twenty minutes then. "I think Kik had enough. So we'll put Kik back home." Carefully lifting the plastic nest, I'd placed it back inside the cat carrier. "Bye Kik."

Situating the nest before the small mirror I'd hung from the carrier's wall, Kiki eyes the bird meeting up with it there.

I'd felt an explanation was in order. "I got a mirror in here. So Kik knows—it can watch itself grow up. And know it's a bird. And not a bleach blonde."

As I'd laughed moronically at my own dumb joke, the bird eyed itself in the mirror. And saw only what it wanted to see. "Eaglet?"

I'd laughed at his ambition. An eaglet? Not. "And so I think that's a good idea." The mirror. "Right Kik?"

The baby wasn't listening, already deep in slumber land.

29

So I'd answered myself. "Right. Goodnight. Goodnight Kik. So there's a mirror in there and Kik looks at himself. Or herself—we can't tell right now." I moved out of the way so Jeff could get a clear shot of the mirror I'd talked about. "Um, if you can get in there and see, there's a little mirror. I don't know whether you can catch that or not."

"Yeah." Jeff saw it, filming inside the carrier now. He'd then moved away so I could close the carrier's door.

But, unable to leave Kiki just yet, I can't do it. I can't quite say goodbye. The door still open, I look back inside one last time. And I'm already worried to leave the bird all alone in there. As if some monster will come along and hurt it when I'm gone.

"Okay, Kik. We'll do this again later. Like in twenty minutes."

The little bird looks out at me, awoken by the screechy noise of the carrier's door being shut. "Don't forget."

I'd make light of what was actually an honored situation. Being a new mother. Getting no sleep. Being stupidly in love.

"Yes, it's all night and all day of great fun. And I love this thing. I do. Goodnight Kik. My little chicken. My little chicken."

I used to have pet chickens that I'd loved immeasurably too. Leg Horns. Plymouth Barred Rocks. Cochins. All birds that I'd lost to old age and missed immeasurably. Missed just like I'd one day miss this little one. The thought of such grief, unbearably unnerving to this love weakened heart.

"Goodnight," I'd said. Still only afternoon, the bird needed to sleep until its next feeding. So I stood back. Finished for now. "There."

Finally shutting the carrier's door, I'd written down what time this feeding took place. Turning to go so the baby could get some much needed shut eye, I'd missed Kiki already. My eyes on the clock, I'd already counted down the minutes until the next feeding. Absence being incredibly hard, it had just been one more hallmark of true love, I'd guessed.

As I left the kitchen, I'd heard Kiki already squeaking for my return. A victim of separation anxiety too—he'd suffered right along with me. Or she'd suffered. Only time would tell what I had here.

But cruelly, time was the only thing we weren't guaranteed to have together.

CHAPTER 2 (VIDEO 2)
FEEDING IN THE DEAD OF NIGHT

June 3, after midnight

That night, I'd dragged myself out of bed at two thirty in the morning. Slipping into the fleece robe that made me look even heavier, I was so glad nobody would see me looking like this.

Pretty well spent, I'd rounded the kitchen doorway with half shut eyes. The infant bird screaming at me from inside its carrier, it was obvious I'd been late. I was in trouble already. To make matters worse, Jeff strolled in behind me—his video camera on again.

"Mom!" Famished, the bird feeling like it was about to die, time was of the essence. "Where have you been?"

Feeling guilty, I'd looked over at the clock, my eyes refusing to focus. "It's two thirty in the morning." Kiki ate four hours ago—the hours seeming like a veritable lifetime to such a tiny baby.

"Hurry!" He squealed incessantly. "Squeak! Squeak! I can't stand it. I'm going to die."

Opening the carrier's door in what seemed like slow motion, I couldn't very well go any faster. Couldn't risk dropping Kiki's little fake nest when trying to get it out. Though I was more tired than ever, I was also happy to see Kiki's face again. This then, having finally perked up.

"There he is." Reaching in to take out Kiki's nest, I say his name over and over, afraid he'd forgotten it since last time. "Kiki.

Kiki. Hi Kik. Hi. Hi Kik. Hi Kiki." My face near his, he'd touched my nose with his open beak.

"I love you. But hurry. Or I'll bite your nose."

A bluff, Kiki would never do such a thing. "Are you going to bite my nose? Are you going to bite my nose?"

His eyes stayed on the syringe as I'd mixed his food with it—the right consistency being everything. "I'm hungry. So very hungry."

Nodding down at him, I feel guilty for not having gotten up sooner. "Yes, good Kik. You're my good Kik." I'd placed his nest safely on the countertop. "There we go." And I'd given him a dollop of food from the syringe.

"Oh no!" Kiki screamed in dread, about to relieve himself. The nub at his back end lifting up, he couldn't clear the tall side of the nest. Then bam! Another disaster.

Dropping the syringe in order to grab a tissue, I was too late. "Uh, oh. Oh. I missed it. I missed it." Our perfectly clean nest was now a mess. "I'll get it. I'll get it."

"My nest isn't a real nest, is it?" He was right. That last try would've worked perfectly, had the nest been real.

The question destroyed me. While Kiki didn't remember his real mother, I was a really hack second best. "I got it. I got it. There, I got it." Holding up my tissue as proof for Jeff, I was proud of helping anyway. "Can you see it?"

Jeff didn't even flinch at the sight of the miniature manure load.

But Kiki had cringed. "Did you get all of it?"

Birds hated having soiled feathers, even at this age. It must've been a survival tactic. A dirty nest being something that would alert predators that a baby lived here perhaps.

"Under control. Under control." I'd grabbed another square and managed to scrape the paper beneath the bird clean. "There. That's the last of it."

I'd tossed the soiled paper into the bag I'd hooked on the half wall separating the kitchen from the basement's stairway. And there, it had joined a zillion others already there, having piled up during the day. That done, I stirred the food in the Dixie cup again. Then drew back the syringe's plunger to fill it.

Kiki needed to be reloaded.

"And now, Kik, there you go, Kik." Lowering the cut tip of the syringe to his beak, I wait for him to open it. "Here goes, Kik."

The nestling, having opened his beak, took the food hungrily. Feeling better already, he looked instantly calmer. "This is good. Yes. Food." After swallowing, the beak popped open again. Kiki, already ready for another round.

He's so adorable when he eats that I go all stupid again. "There goes my Kik." I baby talk to the bird as it eats more because I can't help myself. I'm lost in his little baby bird world. Absolutely lost.

"It's good." As I refill the syringe, Kiki's such a thankful bird. "Thank you, Mom."

Mom. The moniker still had such a charming ring to it. You haven't lived until a newly adopted bird accepts you enough to call you this.

"Kik has to get her beauty rest." Vacillating between calling Kiki a girl or a boy, I'd still been trying to cover all my bases.

"Her?" Kiki had chimed in. "Maybe I'm a guy?"

"*His* beauty rest. He really doesn't, we don't, ah whatever."

It had been so disconcerting not to have the slightest clue as to what gender this bird was. But, I didn't want to hurt anybody's feelings here. And, lowering the food syringe again, it irked me that

I wouldn't know for weeks. I wouldn't know until all the bird's feathers came in. If we were lucky enough to get it to that point. Able to lose him to anything as dumb as an impacted crop or a pasted vent, it was best not to take this tiny little soul for granted. Ever.

Gulping down the food, Kiki beamed up at me. "I'm so glad I'm here. Safe. With you, Mom."

The bird was a heartbreaker all right. "You're my good baby. Yes."

The cuff of my robe accidentally catching on the cat carrier's door, I'd set it rocking a bit. Refilling my syringe, I'm shocked but glad he hadn't been in it at the time. If that had happened, say, when I was trying to put away the nest, I could've dropped him. Shaken, he might've gotten hurt by my own incompetence.

And I know, then and there, that I'm not worthy of being Kiki's mother.

The baby remained unaware of my worries, eying the tube hopefully. "More?"

"Another one?"

I'm so glad the bird's eating, my heart soars again. Sometimes by the time these babies are rescued, they're so run down their appetite is negligible. Their breastbone—sticking out sharply—it's hard to get them back from there. From starvation. With Kiki always being hungry there's hope here, I tell myself. Hope.

"You're my good baby. You're my good baby." Kiki's beak stayed open this time around, I don't know why. And the worry mounts all over again, me thinking I'd done something that hurt him. "Swallow. Swallow. Swallow."

The beak stays open. "No. I'm an eagle."

And I'm alarmed his beak doesn't close. Alarmed that I may have hurt the bird somehow. But it's all for naught when Kiki lifts up its back end, backing into the plastic nest's edge. Struggling to lift his payload over it, he can't again.

"Why is my nest so tall?" Struggling to get to its feet, Kiki doesn't relieve himself this time.

Looking frail and helpless, I can't read his intentions. "Uh, oh. He's not going to do it again, is he?"

Kiki had changed his mind, I guess. "Feed me. I'm almost there."

Feeding the fledgy, I look down at what a marvel it is. "Okay." Having placed the tube into its beak, the bird swallows again. "There." But when I'd neared to feed it with a refilled syringe, the beak had only snapped shut again.

"I'm full."

I hadn't known that. "Oh, we're tapped. We're not…" Hungry anymore. "It's enough. All right. It's enough." Repeating all this, it wasn't because Kiki wasn't listening. I'd just blathered on because I was spellbound by him. In love with him. Reeling in my emotions, I move on. "Okay." Out to get in one more syringe, I'd only done it in the hopes I could sleep in a little later. "So, this will hold it till four in the morning." I could hope it would anyway.

"You will come back, right?" Kiki had fears that needed to be slaked.

"And I'll be back at four in the morning." Kiki took another beakful of food just to please me. "Okay. Here you go. There you go. Oh, there's my little, Kik. Come on. Oh. He's had enough. Kik's had enough." I kiss the top of Kiki's little head. "I'll see you at four. Can you hold on till four? Four?" I didn't think I could myself. "In the meantime you can just work on your pin feathers? If I was you I would. Because, really, nobody's gonna do it for you. Really. In life, you're just going to have to do things yourself sometimes. And I think you should start there."

"You think so?" The tiny bird scrutinized my face. And then it looked down at his own feeble looking feathers.

"I do. It's good advice."

"Do I have to start now? I'm tired."

"Like, maybe in the morning. Your tail could use some work." Nearly nonexistent, it was only about an eighth of an inch long. The actual feathers being a long way off, his laughable tail was still more butt nub than anything else.

"Is my tail going to be important?"

I'd say. "You're going to need it. So I would start there. I would. All right?" Always waking up before me, he'd need something to think about. To work at. Till next time.

Kiki had remained mute, thinking this over.

"Okay, hmm?" I couldn't believe I didn't want to leave the bird again. "And I'll see you at four?"

"Four's good for me."

We'd kissed goodnight again. "Get your beauty rest."

"Beauty? And if I'm a boy bird?"

Boy birds were just as gorgeous, if not more so. "Get your beauty rest, Kiki." Lifting his nest ever so carefully, I'd slid it back into the carrier. Making sure I'd put him down before his mirror, his unsure eyes stayed on mine.

"But...?"

"Bye Kik. See you at four. Bye Kik. There you go. Okay."

Yawning, I'd left the kitchen, though reluctantly. I had a hard time leaving him stranded there. All alone. But really, if I didn't start getting some shut-eye, I'd be heading off a cliff tomorrow.

I called back to the miniature life form locked inside the big cat carrier. "Goodnight." And I missed the bird already, worried for it.

Dead tired, once I was back in bed and snug under my covers, I couldn't nod off despite being exhausted. The anxiety mounting, what if I'd slept through the next feeding?

Then, having taken hours to fall back asleep, I'd only slept about a half hour before having to get back up again. Wondering how long I could go on this way, I promised myself I would do it. For Kiki's sake.

But there was always this single, dark realization about Kiki that always kept me awake at night. Always mowed down my happiness when I'd least expected it to. And this was that thought.

These precious moments that we shared being so fleeting, each one could always be our last.

CHAPTER 3 (VIDEO 3)
OUR FIRST WALK OUTSIDE

June 4, noon

A day later, I'd thrown on a blue jean skirt and a white cotton shirt.
Being all dressed up—for me that is—today would be a great
occasion. It would be the day Kiki and I would take our first walk
together. Outside. To discuss the reality of what kind of bird he truly
might be.

An eagle not being an option.

Once out the door, I'd held my hand over Kiki's nest like a
parent flamingo holds its wing over a nestling. Then, moving across
the grass on wobbly legs, I'd been worried I'd hit a mole hole. And
go down. Pecking my way out to a park bench in the pine garden, I
had other concerns too.

Very scared my new baby could jump out of its nest and hop
away, I'd remained overly cautious. But I had to do bring him
outside. If Kiki was ever going to be a free bird, he'd need to be
acclimated to the great outdoors sooner or later.

As it was, the bird sunk down in its nest. It was frightened of the
sun overhead. Of the sounds of birds all around us. Of the immense
blue patch of nothingness over its head.

As I sat down on the bench, Kiki stayed like that, all ducked
down in his plastic nest. His eyes on the sun, directly overhead, as
light dappled through the pine boughs. And here, I'd planned on our
having our first real heart to heart talk.

Wondering what kind of bird I had here, the possibilities seemed endless. He was gray. Just gray. All gray. Everything. Even his irises.

Those eyes unused to be outside, Kiki shut them against the bright sun. All hunkered down, he didn't make a peep either. But when he opened his eyes again and looked around inquisitively, he'd finally relaxed. Worried for nothing.

"So, what do you want to be when you grow up?"

"An eagle." Kiki showed no hesitation. "I'll be really big. With a six foot wing span. You'll see."

At this point, with Kiki weighing only a few ounces, his dream seemed ridiculous. Though only about a week and a half old by now, anyone could plainly see that he was destined to remain some sort of itsy bitsy songbird. Yet, his certainty broke my heart.

I couldn't very well tell him the truth. That he'd never amount to becoming anything remotely close to an eagle. The truth being that he was most likely a small blackbird. Average. Common. A grackle, perhaps. But I figured I'd steer the conversation somewhere else, sort of like a good salesperson would. And in so doing, this little heart with the big aspirations wouldn't be needlessly broken.

"You're going to keep your options open?" I'd insisted.

The bird sat up a little higher in the nest. "Why should I?"

"Are you?"

Pressing on, Kiki didn't take the hint I'd been nearly forcing upon him. Her. With Kiki not even knowing what kind of bird he was himself yet, and me stuck in the rut of not knowing if he was male or female—we had a problem. Sometimes I called him one thing. Sometimes another. And yet, he was always sure he was an eaglet.

"You're going to keep your options open?"

"I'm not a songbird," Kiki had insisted to me. "I'm an eagle."

An eagle.

So there it was. I could hem and haw and skirt the issue till the cows came home. But Kiki was sure about that.

"No way." I knew this conversation would eventually go here. I had an inkling Kiki wouldn't give up this dream easily. "You want to be what? An eagle?"

I peered down at the weak, tiny nestling in its fake human-made nest. Right now, thinking it would most likely grow up to be a grackle, we were at a painful impasse. Finding out Kiki's lofty aspirations, hearing the truth may prove to be devastating for him. And this is the type of bird person who would not take kindly to finding it out it may be regarded as *common*. Nobody would like finding that out.

But that is what a common grackle would be. Common.

I'd let him down gently. "I'm not sure an eagle is right for you. How about, say—a grackle? Grackles are good." I could tell he didn't think much of this idea. "Starlings? Starlings are good. Even a cedar waxwing."

"They wear masks. Eagles don't wear masks. When I grow up, I'll be an eagle."

"You want to be an eagle."

My statement having fallen on even flatter ears, I still didn't want to dash Kiki's high hopes. To aspire to be a Bald Eagle would be tantamount to aspiring to be a hero. And didn't we all strive to become more than what we were born to be? Being taught we could attain anything we tried when we grew up, Kiki was no different. He felt if he'd only tried hard enough. Could fly far enough. He could be whatever he wanted to be. But for his sake, Kiki's, my thoroughly American bird, he had to be forced into seeing reality somehow.

Without getting hurt in the process, of course.

I pressed on, offering other options. "I mean, a turkey vulture?" These birds have big wingspans. And Kiki could certainly pass for a baby vulture, the sides of his head still being naked, crimson flesh. "No? How about something smaller than that? How about, a grackle? Or a catbird?"

There it is. I'd said it. Out loud.

Kiki wouldn't hear of it. "Just because I'm gray? And they're gray?"

"I'm thinking a catbird. I'm thinking—why not?"

The baby bird only shook its head. "And I'm thinking, no way."

"What do you…?"

Kiki had interrupted me. "Eagle."

"What?" Stunned he wouldn't let this idea go, it appeared I'd already lost the war of wills with the bird.

"I want to be an eagle. An eagle. Not a grackle."

My heart sank to my stomach. Feeling queasy, I was pretty sure I had an obstinate male bird here. A bird who'd pinned all of his pin feathers on becoming this impossible dream. If he hung on to this pipe dream, the painful truth would become apparent in just a few short weeks. Because that's when all his feathers would unfurl. And when that happened, this two ounce weakling would be in for one big major heartache.

To spare him, I'd nip this fantasy in the bud. And right now too. "No." As in no way you're ever growing up to be an eagle.

"Mom?" Kiki had looked up at me, hurt filling his eyes. "Not a grackle. Never a grackle."

I'd decided I must let him down gracefully. Eyeing the top of its dark head, the bird could at least hear other ideas. "I'm sure of it. I'm sure of it. I'm sure a grackle. Or catbird. Maybe even a starling."

Kiki could hang out with starlings, yes. Never an eagle though. Too dangerous. They'd look at him like I looked at a dessert cart—drooling.

"There's starlings around here for you to play with." Looking around for starlings, not one is around.

"Excuse me? Starlings have orange legs. Mine? They're dark. Nope. Not a starling."

I didn't know whether this statement was true or not, making a mental note to look up starlings in my Audubon bird book.

I'd pressed courageously onward. "Starlings could be the thing for you. There's tons of them. And they're everywhere. But I like catbirds. They're in the mulberry trees. I got a lot of mulberry trees."

"My mind, it's made up. I'm an eaglet."

I repeat myself, hoping Kiki will see the light. "I got a lot of mulberry trees. You like that. Yes? I love you." There. That should stop all this nonsense. I'd love Kiki no matter what he—or she—would end up being.

"I love you more. But I'm still a baby eagle."

"I know." My heart broken, how could I let this wacky idea persist? Why couldn't he aim for being something smaller? Something more attainable? "Kiki. Come on, now. You could be anything you want. It's true. The sky is the limit. The sky is the limit, Kik." Looking up at the great blue expanse over our heads, it sure seemed possible. That Kiki could be anything at all.

As long as that something was a grackle or catbird or starling.

"Mom? I want to be what I want to be. An eagle."

When all was said and done, I didn't have the heart to quash his hopes at such a tender age. So I'd opted for changing the subject. Like that would work.

43

"All right then. Let's go in and eat. What do you think? You want to?"

Kiki remained mute. Like he'd realized exactly what I'd just tried to do.

Restless myself, my legs are itching to go back inside before an actual eagle flies over the house. Which they always did. The house being that near to the Mississippi River. Where they'd congregated to fish, even in summer.

"What do you think? Should we go in and eat?" Still getting the cold wing, I could not believe this. "Should we?"

"I'm an eaglet."

"We could stay out here. It's beautiful out. Quite beautiful out."

Kiki looked around, assessing his place in the world. "Being a big, bad eagle—I could stay out here alone."

The tiny baby having no idea how cruel this world could be, he'd be an instant meal for somebody. A passing hawk. A barn cat. And yes, an *eagle*.

Him out to befriend the enemy, this notion I'd have to kibosh post haste. "No. You're not ready. Don't worry. Soon you'll be ready. And everything will go better for you then. You'll find a mate. Birds are well known for loving their mate. I mean, they mate for life. And you'll have eggs. And it'll be such fun. I mean, really there's nothing better than to live outside. And fly around with the birds."

"As an eagle. Not some small bird."

Now I'd done it. Using psychology on this pure little entity, one incapable of lying, was proving to be tricky. But with eagles only able to roost in humongous trees, Kiki would have more options being small.

"Think of the trees you could live in. The trees alone would be worth it. I mean, you could almost perch now too." We'd been practicing, trying to get Kiki to stand on my finger. And he'd almost gotten it. "So this is a good thing. And, I would just, I would just wing it…"

"As an eagle. I'll stay out here. Alone."

"…and see how it goes from there." This big shot needed to know he wasn't yet ready. But I'd let him know how wonderful it would be like when it got older. And could stay out by himself. "At first, if you're scared, you can come back in the house. Or we can, I don't know, put you in a flight cage. Or…"

Or nothing. All fledglings have to start out in a flight cage. It's better Kiki knew that right now.

I'd press him into this thought gently. "Flight cages are good. I've used those before. And birds like them. And the only thing we need to do is make sure you're eating. On your own. Before we put you outside. Because if you're not, we can't put you outside. So, perching is good. Eating is good. And you got to work on your thigh muscles. Because when you fly, your thigh muscles are everything. I mean, takeoffs are good. Takeoffs are easy—I hear. It's the landings that are the thing." Or so I'd read many human pilots have said.

"All eagles land good."

Why did I ever open my big mouth at all? "Landings are amazingly hard."

"Even for an eagle?"

"Well, you heard it here first. You heard it here first. But, okay so, landings are hard. But we'll work on flying."

"I can probably fly already, me being an eaglet."

Kiki couldn't even stand yet, let alone fly. Nowhere near being fully feathered, this poor little thing sure had impossible dreams.

45

God, I so loved this little guy. Girl. Whatever. I'd really have to bulk him up first though before we attempted anything foolish. And soon.

The sun getting too hot, I think our time outside should end. "Let's go in and eat."

"You think I can't fly yet?"

I'd thought he'd needed to eat. "Let's just do it—I can tell you want to eat."

"What I want is to be an eagle."

"Okay. I know. Well, you said so. You said it yourself." But I was still in charge, being the only mother Kiki had right now. And as such, I had command of the plastic nest. "Okay. Let's go."

Grasping Kiki's only home firmly, I'm once again afraid I'll trip and drop him. Regardless, we'd stood up under the fragrant cedar trees, the sun warming both our faces. His nest held close to my own, we'd walked down the path for the front door. And as I'd walked, I had to wonder about all this eagle business.

Maybe Kiki, still a mere baby, had been playing make-believe. Like any other kid would. But if he wasn't, at release time, he had to admit he wasn't an eagle. For, seeking them out would mean the end of him.

And me.

CHAPTER 4 (VIDEO 4)
KIKI AND I TEAM UP

June 4, afternoon

Since first arriving at my front door, Kiki had become my best bud now. His nest was now inside a huge cat carrier on a folding table, I'd set it up in my own bedroom. Becoming roommates, we'd grown closer than ever.

By now, I was almost positive Kiki was a budding guy bird. He really spent all his time by his mirror, which male birds always did. I don't know why. Don't know if they were picking a fight with the other bird. Or just admiring themselves.

Probably a week old when I first saw Kiki's tiny face, he was probably about two weeks old now. Still, two weeks is kind of young to hang on to his lofty eagle aspirations. An eagle. Jeesh. Then I'd found out that Kiki had even more things in his little head to accomplish.

Besides wanting to be an eagle, Kiki thought we should write a book together.

A lot of work dead ahead, I'd only agreed for one reason alone. Kiki would be at my side during the whole process. Or on my shoulder. Or sitting on my head. Luckily, Kiki had learned to perch the day before. He'd loved the perch I'd made him from a beautiful downed birch branch. The perch being three inches wide and one inch tall, I'd made it with a hacksaw and a glue gun. The fledgling having plunked down on it, he waited intently on the table next to my computer.

Alone at the desk in my room, surrounded by vases of roses, our time together had grown beyond precious. The fate we would suffer at his release one awful day, and soon, the thought loomed ever large for us both. So for every second of every minute, of every hour—life was treasured. Release was a harrowing event for anyone. Anything awful that could happen—would happen.

And with this little guy insisting he was an eagle, anything might happen.

I'd once adored a baby crow at the wildlife center, weeks spent rehabbing it. When it came time for the director to release this crow, it had flown directly into the path of an oncoming car. Striking a motorist's windshield, the bird died instantly. And because I'd grieved terribly to this day for having lost that friend, I never wanted to see that happen again. Especially to my Kiki.

Therefore, all the time Kiki and I spent together proved to be beyond treasured. With his having to fly off one day into the great unknown, and soon, I'd be left an empty nester. A real one. So, we'd thusly began our task of getting our lives down on paper. And with heavy hearts too.

Having been fed, the baby bird lounged peacefully on its birch perch as I typed away. It was amazing, how his eyes followed the words moving across the screen. The pinpoint precision would be good practice though—for when Kiki would have to hunt bugs to survive. Like kids playing video games acquire good hand-eye coordination, watching the words might help Kiki's beak-eye coordination.

Suddenly, Kiki's head did a one hundred eighty degree turn. His gaze fastening on the door at our backs, I then saw movement out of the corner of my eye too. Both recognizing who'd entered through the doorway, Jeff, the cameraman-slash-husband, had sneaked in. And if there's one thing I hate more than getting my picture taken—it's being filmed when I hadn't expected to be filmed.

Setting the floorboards to squeaking, Jeff slid past my white metal canopy bed and neared us. His lens filming my sanctuary, my very room, I'd felt hideously invaded. Everything would be on easy display here. My lavender walls. My turn of the century wire dress form that looked like something out of Cinderella. My pale green French Country desk. The giant metal vases of roses sitting on the floor flanking either side of it.

But after a few prickly seconds had elapsed, Kiki and I both calmed down and pensively decided to greet him cordially.

Turning to face my husband with a smile, I'd been glad I'd put on my nicest white linen shirt. Then I began our introduction.

"Hi. Me and Kiki..." I'd felt compelled to introduce my star—the littlest, but most glaring, light of my life. "This is Kiki. Kik's looking at the words he's just writing." And me having said that proved my grammar was worse than his. "Kik is writing a book. It's called Kiki and The Bird Whisperer. Uh, for now."

Since the fledgy and I had yet to discuss anything but a working title, I hated to step on such tiny feet. But by the way Kiki looked at me, I think I already had.

"Hi, Kik." Picking up the food syringe, I'd asked Kiki with body language if he was ready to eat.

"Yes, please." Kiki eyed the food in my hand.

Watching him swallow, chills had run up my spine. I still felt lucky every time he was famished. At the wildlife center, so many little birds came in poisoned by pesticides and herbicides, their livers were too taxed to ever heal. Jaundiced with yellow skin, they wouldn't eat at all. They couldn't even hold their heads up. Feeding them against their will, hoping against all reason that they'd pull through, they had no swallowing reflex. Sitting there until they'd died, seeing voracious fledglings always seemed like a miracle.

I smiled at my little hungry eaglet—my soul at peace by now with who he'd wanted to be. An eagle. Okay. All right. Anything— as long as he didn't up and die on me.

I'd fed the fledgling, still an honor to do so. "There you go. Go ahead, swallow. Swallow, swallow." I laughed when he did, so proud of him. Such was my pure bliss at how he still seemed healthy. "So we're writing this book together." Or so I'd told our intruder—Jeff.

Adrenaline rushed through Kiki. He was almost as excited as when he got to eat a meal worm. "Tell how in the book they will get to hear what I'm saying. My idea, too."

The whole thing having been Kiki's idea, I'd sat thinking. Who'd believe a bird wanted such a thing? I'd take baby steps into the truth. "He's got a lot of input. Um, you know like, just things like I don't really know." There I was, babbling again.

Kiki had added real input just then. Out to help, he always seemed more level headed than I under pressure. "Just start at the beginning. Tell how all of this happened. How we met."

But put on the spot abruptly, I still didn't know how to begin. "Um, the way he was abandoned by his mother, how that happened. And what it felt like. These things are—I can't make it up. I can't make it up."

"Pick me up? So I can be closer to you?"

Carefully lifting him off his perch, his little black feet wrapped around my finger. "So Kik is helping me. Kik's at the computer and we're just gonna, we were just writing about Seal Team Six just now. And um, and how…"

Kiki shoots me a look. Then he unexpectedly wobbles on my finger as if unsure of something I'd said.

I'd looked at the bird. "Was it something I said? We're writing about how they, if you really want to know how it feels to be abandoned somewhere. Like in-country. Or, something funny like that."

Kiki had opened his beak then touched it to my lips. "Funny like being abandoned after falling out of a nest?"

Sitting red faced, what had I been thinking? "But it's not funny to be abandoned." I'd backtrack but it was too late, the damage done. "Not *funny*. But you know what I mean."

Kiki touches my face again. "There's something else."

"And—what?" I'd listened intently but the bird got silent again, thinking something through. "What?" I demand.

Kiki quietly touches my forehead, laying out his idea for the book's premise. "It could work."

"Oh, no." I wasn't too keen on his idea, not even wanting to mention it.

But Kiki grew insistent. "Jeff, he read us a story about it last night." The internet news. I thought Kiki had been dozing. "We got to add them to the story."

"Really?" I'd still had my doubts.

Kiki ran his beak down the center of my nose to get my full attention. "I want them in the story."

At the mercy of this fad Kiki was all jazzed about, I caved. "I wasn't aware of that. All right. We can add that." I'd turned to Jeff to unload everything that Kiki had just demanded. "He wants to put zombies in the book." Zombies, for God's sake. Something I'd known nothing about. "So, all right, we'll put zombies in the book."

Kiki's gaze remained fastened on the computer's screen. He was searching for a place to insert the idea, no doubt.

Having been overwhelmed by the idea, what did zombies have to do with me having adopted Kiki? And I'd told him as much. "I have no idea what it does with your story."

"Work it in. Just try. You afraid of zombies?"

Real funny. "I'm not sure. About all of it." Zombies. This was so dumb.

"Please?"

Kiki's wide eyes on me, I sat wondering where I could possibly insert the walking dead into a book about a glorious little bird. Still, I'd acquiesced. And it wasn't just to shut him up either. I was a sucker for whatever Kiki wanted to do. Out to please him first and foremost, I had my reasons. Our time together—ever looming shorter and shorter.

And, well, his enthusiasm was catchy. "Okay, I can do it. I can do it. I'm a writer. I can." Though I'd doubted I could, I would certainly try. For Kiki's sake.

His eyes on me distrustfully, he hadn't believed me. "Promise?"

"Trust me. If you want zombies, you got them. You got zombies."

But the bird didn't trust me. At all. "Mom?" Gray eyes honing in on mine, he was out to make sure I'd add zombies. "It's all over the internet. Zombie this. Zombie that."

I'd concede, zombies being big for some time now. "All right. All right."

"And make them insects too. The zombies. It'll be fun for us birds."

Kiki must've thought that people would read his book to their parakeets.

I'd make sure I'd understood this concept. "It's like—meal worm zombies?"

"Yes. Meal worm zombies."

I'd explain this all for Jeff's sake. "That's the closest thing he can come to. Is a meal worm as a zombie."

Kiki had nodded. "Meal worms. Blech! They squirm around in your crop like crazy. It's like that guy in the movie Alien. You think they'll bust out. Kill you at any moment."

I'd done a mental shudder. "Okay." My blood pressure rising off the charts, my room seemed like it had been getting hotter. "Meal worms can be in the story."

"But…" Kiki looked away for a second then back at me. "Meal worm zombies."

"I promise. I'll put meal worm zombies in the story. I know, it's interesting." To birds. "And, people need to know these things."

Kiki relaxed. "Can we hug? I mean, to seal the deal?"

Placing my whole face against his tiny baby bird body, my nerves immediately calmed. "So that's what we're going to do. We're going to write our story."

Kiki had another question. "And then—after we write it?"

I was out to slake his fears about distribution. "And we're going to put it out for people to read. And it'll be fun."

Kiki seemed to have calmed down a lot. "Other birds might like my zombie book."

His softly feathered body so near my eyes, I could view him with ease. "Other birds might be able to be interested. If somebody reads it to them."

The baby bird nodded. "A story for the birds."

And so we were in agreement. "And so that's what we'll do. We're just going to keep going on this. And we'll, you know, just pound away." Me actually doing all the typing though, I should feel a little put upon, doing all the real work here. "And sooner or later, it'll be a story." I'd known the process by now all right. Typing stuff for hours on end till a story emerged.

Kiki looked back at the computer, waiting. "Make the words dance there again."

I'd laughed, an absolute honor to write about a baby bird as wonderful as my baby bird. "Kiki! Kiki!" I was so thankful to have him right now, I could have just burst.

He'd checked the words on the screen. "Let's get back to work. Where were we then?"

Pointing at the computer screen, I'd shown him where we'd left off. "We were right here. If you wanted to know."

"Wait! About a bird, the story's got to have flying." That said, Kiki jumped off my finger. Unable to fly yet, he'd crashed into the vase of yellow roses on my desk. His beak pressing their petals, he tried to save face. "I just wanted to be in them, the roses."

"All right. Okay." Making the bird sit on my finger, I'd stick to his alibi. "It's important to be in the roses. It's important to be in the roses because he likes being in roses. So there you go."

"I'm usually a good bird, right?"

"Isn't he a good bird?" Perched dutifully on my finger, he could never be a bad bird. "Kik! Kiki!"

"Mom. I know why you say my name so much. I won't forget your voice. When I'm out there."

I'd hoped he wouldn't. Because his scratchy little bird voice—I would never forget. Never.

I'd hoped we'd remember each other so that when we'd both departed this world, we'd find each other again in heaven. The love in your heart the only thing you can bring with you, the only thing read by The Lord, He'd have to know that we should be together forever. Me and Kiki. The thought made me jittery.

"Mom, hold still." Kiki's legs were unstable on my index finger.

But I marvel only at his ability to stand at all. "He's perching now beautifully."

"Will you teach me to fly—tomorrow?"

I reeled his hopes back in towards reality. A ways to go on that score, I wouldn't dash his dream entirely. "So we'll probably get a flight cage now." But Kiki would have to know how to do a few things first before he lived in such a big cage. "If he eats on his own."

Which he still wasn't doing yet.

Holding the bird absent mindedly over my keyboard, I still couldn't figure out how parent birds got their babies weaned. I'd found it a nearly impossible task. To starve the baby in the hopes it would feed itself just wasn't in me. I think the key may be to give it an enticing assortment of things to peck at. Soft yellow corn kernels. Hard cooked egg yolk. Mulberries.

"I'll eat on my own. I will."

But he hadn't even tried yet. "He's going to have to eat on his own," I reiterate. With all this talk of food, something dawned on me. "And I might as well remove him from the keyboard." Knowing he was due for a doodle, I would sure have a mess on my hands, if that happened.

"Why?" Kiki erroneously thought he was in complete control of his bodily functions by now.

I couldn't believe he'd asked that. "Because accidents happen. Right?"

"I'm not a hatchling anymore."

It's like he'd said himself. "Doodle happens."

Kiki laughed. He flapped his wings gently against my face till I laughed too. "Me and Mom. Just like that poet you told me about."

And so we were. "We can do a really mean Edgar Allen Poe impersonation too. He really wants to be a raven, Kiki." But it seemed I'd put words in his mouth—beak

For he'd quickly set me straight on that score. "An eagle."

I'd pressed on, pulling his leg. "Ravens are his thing right now."

"You wish."

I'd joke harder. "He wanted to be—he saw a cardinal outside. And thought he'd wanted to be a cardinal."

"Ugh. Liar." Kiki pecked under his wing, out to ignore any further suggestions.

I plowed on, keeping up the charade to irk him. "And everyday, it's a little something else. You know how kids are."

"Not this kid." The baby had touched his beak against my nose. "It's eagle all the way."

I wouldn't upset him now, writing to do. "Okay. All right." We kissed. "Okay?"

"I love you, Mom."

"I know."

The computer screen at Kiki's back having just gone dark, the change had frightened him. "Where'd the words go?"

"Well, oops, see what happened?" I'd hit the machine's spacebar to light things up again.

Kiki looked behind himself, his fears still not slaked. "Should we hurry?"

"Okay, let's just keep going. We're just going to keep going and um, you know. I'm adding zombies. So…" I hear Jeff laugh. "If he says vampires, I won't believe it." Meaning, if the bird knows that my other books, Hypnotic and Magnetic, were vampire stories— well. Wouldn't that just have been too weird? "But okay, I can add a zombie."

Kiki's jumps right in. "Vampires."

Laughing at how funny he could be, the bird sure did pay attention to everything happening around him.

And he'd laughed right along with me. "I do listen in!"

"I know. I know. Okay." With a smile, I'd placed my hand beneath him in case he was about to have an accident. Without him knowing I had done it, of course.

The bird and I had looked off into each others eyes for a few seconds. We liked just hanging out together all day long. Moments like these, making me grieve for how short and fleeting our lives together would be. Soon his tail nub would fill in with feathers. The baby down sticking out all over his head would be replaced by sleek black feathers. His body would grow to match his huge baby beak, still impossibly big for his head.

"I'll miss you too." Kiki had managed to read my mind again. "But my head, it'll be white."

A white eagle's head.

I'd hugged Kiki under my chin. "Yeah. I know, Sweetie." Time to get back to work, I'd been thankful for something to change the subject. Raising him up onto my right shoulder, I'd found just the thing. "You on my shoulder, we'll write like this then."

Up by my ear, I'd heard a quiet whisper. "I could stay here forever."

But I knew he couldn't. "That's okay." An impossibility, I'd forgotten where I was in my life. Let alone in the story we were writing. Placing my fingers against the keyboard, I perused the screen with unsure eyes. "Where was I?"

"Zombies."

"Whoop!" How could I have forgotten that tidbit? "All right." I'd started to add them for Kiki's sake. "Zombies. Zombies." But the bird got all my attention again. "Kiki. Kiki." I loved him so. Typing away, I'd quickly kept my promise to Kiki. There. "Zombies are added."

Kiki, laughing in my ear, he'd sounded like a little quacking duck. Nuzzling his body against my face, a small hurricane of love ripped across the pit of my stomach. Knowing I'd miss him someday, the feeling of his being here like this, it was all too bittersweet. With a heavy heart, I'd felt his beak near my ear.

"I'm right here, Mom. Right here."

"Okay." His sincerity heartbreakingly advanced for a mere baby, I'd decided to make him laugh. "What are you doing back there?"

"I'm telling you I love you."

Stunned, I'd wondered if Jeff had picked up on this. "He's whispering in my ear," I'd said to him.

Kiki's voice grew fainter. "I won't want to fly away, when the time comes. I won't."

"Oh?" Kiki's admission cutting me to the bone, the devastation made my hands go to jelly.

"We should put it in the book, Mom. How we feel."

"All right."

After laying out a few more ideas, Kiki seemed tired. "Thirsty. Tired. But I still want to see outside."

I'd told Jeff what the fledgy had said. "He needs some water. And then, he wants to go back outside to look at the sky for a while. So maybe we'll do that."

Kiki rubbed his head on my shoulder, nuzzling me. "I'll stay on your shoulder. We could watch the clouds change. Wait for eagles. And…"

"And, I don't know." I'd smiled at his perseverance. But he'd stand corrected just the same. "Just have some fun."

The pain of letting go of this smart little bundle of brains some day already seemed an impossibility. I couldn't fathom parting with him, Kiki. Not now. Not ever. Not even for a minute.

Let alone for forever.

Knowing what could happen upon the release of a wild bird from captivity, it was all I could do to not cry. But the bird already wanted to be outside. The sky—his. Typing for a few seconds more, I'd abruptly stopped. Trying to maintain a cheerful façade, my stomach was actually in knots. But I'd smiled and pretended I was all right. For his sake.

"All done."

But I knew. I knew that Kiki's book would be the hardest thing I'd ever done in my entire life. Already unbearable, trying to put our lives into words, I wasn't even sure it could be done. So much about his release, being weeks off, burnt with pain already. I just couldn't look forward to the day, the hour, the minute, the second I'd have to say goodbye to him.

And after he was gone, Kiki, how would I ever watch one of his videos? How could I watch one when I wouldn't know where in the world he'd gone off to? When I wouldn't know what had actually happened to him?

When I wouldn't know if he'd survived or not?

No. I couldn't watch these tiny snippets of his life pass through my eyes like so much meaningless light. For to do so, being left irreparably torn apart by the experience, I'd never be whole again. My heart then, forever with Kiki wherever he may end up, will be my parting gift to him. Because really, I'd already given it without having meant to do so. I gave him my heart the very first moment I'd laid eyes on his baby self.

An adoptive mother's love—no less striking than any other.

CHAPTER 5 (VIDEO 5)
BIRD MUG SHOTS

June 4, late afternoon

A few days later, my dear Kiki asked for help in remembering his birth mother. Or, more succinctly—his egg mother. As her identity had remained a fuzzy mystery to him. Well, feathery anyhow.

Seizing the opportunity, it would be the perfect time to present other options to him. So many choices being just as good as becoming an eagle.

Naturally, like any adopted child, Kiki wondered what she must have looked like, his real mother. He'd wondered how old she'd been when she laid his egg. Once, cutting through the living room, his eyes had landed on Dovey. My female dove. So I'd asked if he thought his mother looked like her. Shaking his head no, he'd said *that's not her. But I think her head was white too.* And I'd felt so terrible for him. The whole eagle identity crisis still weighing so heavily on his young mind.

He'd so wanted her to be an eagle, his mother, with all his heart.

Still, our writing done for this particular day, we'd decided to find out who she could've been. By the looks of Kiki at this point in time, once could easily believe that his mother could've been a vulture. With the sides of his head still being pink and bald. With the tufts of baby down sticking out. If vultures would stay only about as big as a robin, he might've been able to fool anyone.

Kiki sat waiting on his little birch perch at the folding table I'd set up in my room. Holding the Audubon bird book before him, we'd peruse it together. Me being the one with hands, fingers, Kiki found me of the utmost use sometimes. The both of us smiling at Jeff when he'd showed up, we watching him make a slow approach. Jeff again horning in on our little chat, I'd watched him shrug. As if saying *what are you two doing now?*

I'd told Jeff exactly what we were doing now, me and Kiki. "Well, you know, we're looking through the Audubon book for his mother. It's bird mug shots. And so we're trying to find his mom." Turned to a page full of black birds, I'd looked down at the little bird to make sure he was paying attention.

Kiki looked over each photo before his beak. "I didn't know this would be so exhausting."

"And um, he's been tired. You know, it's just like anything. Looking through that many pictures, it just makes you tired. And uh, but he did, he did think it was this one. Right, right? Did you think it was this one?" I pointed to the photo of the grackle.

Kiki having thought nothing of the sort, he stood restlessly on his perch. Eyes honing in on the photo, he'd touched the exact photo with his beak. Then he stretched his wings up in a big, hard to miss, shrug. "If she had a white head and tail—maybe."

The head and tail of a bald eagle.

I'd lie for his sake, cajoling him ever nearer the truth. "Yeah, yeah. This one looked familiar."

Kiki would have none of it. "She's no eagle, that bird."

"Um." I stopped there. I knew he wouldn't want to hear this. "It's a *common* grackle." Knowing this would catch in his craw—or crop—I'd done a mental cringe.

"Common?" The word had made Kiki wince. "But I'm not common."

"He's not sure," I'd fibbed.

Kiki would have none of this grackle business. "I don't remember her, my real mother. It doesn't matter anyway. I have you. You're enough mother for me, right?"

I knew denial when I heard it, but I'd give him that. "He's not sure. He was really just an egg at the time. He was barely out. And um, he thinks maybe this." I show him another photo, hoping the bird will keep a more open mind.

Pecking at his tail, he'd blown off my suggestion completely. "My eyes were still closed. Maybe I'm that other bird, the one we looked at earlier."

I explain. "He also saw the picture of a gray catbird. He thought the gray catbird looked an awful—well, oh. Look at that!"

"Look at me!" Kiki, using misdirection, had stood up on his legs. For the first time ever. And all in an effort to change the subject.

"He turned into a transformer." Shocked, I'd never known how tall he was before this moment.

"I looked tall, right? Like an eagle?"

I sat transfixed. "When he stands up, he transforms into a transformer." Knowing he'd only stood up to deflect me off my grackle course, I'd try to play along. "Okay. Okay. Did you want to look at the catbird again?"

"Turn to the eagle page."

This again. "Did you…?" I had no idea what I'd wanted to ask him.

"You heard me."

I shook my head. "Not the eagle. No."

63

Kiki would fight for his integrity. "Tell everybody the truth."

I didn't want to go there, for his sake. But I give up all at once. "He maintains he could have an eagle father."

Kiki stood his ground, there on his birch perch. "Which makes me an eaglet."

Sitting flummoxed, I looked over to Jeff. "You know, I told him these things can't happen." That a grackle mother couldn't possible hatch an eagle baby. "But, he's hoping."

"Please, Mom. Think about the parades I could do."

Jeff needed to know what this all meant. "He really wants to be an eagle because he would like to be patriotic. He would like to do parades on the Fourth of July. And things of this nature. There's one eagle he saw on TV that, right…?" The TV being my computer screen.

Kiki got excited at the thought. "The eagle that flies around the stadium?"

"Oh yeah, that one, yeah."

"I want to be like him, Mom." That was Kiki. Full of impossible ambition.

"That's exactly the one I'm talking about. The eagle that was, he does like football games?"

"And baseball games."

I'd nodded. "And baseball games. He flies all over the, the um." Darn it. The word had escaped me. "The auditorium."

Kiki shot me a duh look. "It's not called an auditorium when it's outside."

Standing corrected, put on the spot by a bird, I couldn't think straight. "No. It's not an auditorium. What is that call…baseball field?"

"I thought mothers were invincible?"

Kids. I'd laughed, mystified by him as ever. "I never said I knew anything about sports."

"Lets wonder why. If we'd watched the games..."

"Well, okay. We can watch the game sometimes." That is if I found replays on the internet, not owning a television set anymore. "Who, who do you like?"

"The Sox."

"The Sox?" I could've almost heard my immediate ancestors from the North Side of Chicago turning over in their respective graves. This little one needed to be steered into the truth. "No, no, no. Cubs maybe? Cubs?"

"I'm thinking more like the Cardinals?" And he'd probably thought that was a team of birds. "The Baltimore Orioles?"

I sat wondering where Kiki had gotten all this from. Jeff. There was the real culprit. "Well, all right then. But..."

Kiki interrupted me. "Or that team from Cincinnati."

"The Cincinnati Reds?" I'd plow forward, pretending to know what I was talking about. "No. That team from Boston that does so well. You like them."

"Sox." Kiki, as stubborn as Jeff about baseball, was trying to irk me.

I'd moved on reluctantly. "Okay." Pointing at the book again, I'd steer this conversation the way I'd wanted it to go. "So here's this. We can, we can once..."

"Mom, if I'm not a grackle, can I be something else?"

"What?" I had to ask.

"One of those crazy birds. A cuckoo bird. That's it."

I was sure Kiki was no such thing. "No, I don't, I don't think so."

Then it dawns on me, what Kiki's trying to pull here. Shocked speechless that a baby bird has pulled my chain, I play along.

I'd looked down at his minute self. "Are you sure? All right. Let me go back. Let me go back." Finding the right page, I tried to set him straight. "The cuckoo bird?"

"Yep. The cuckoo bird."

"You're definitely…" He's no way a cuckoo bird. But it appeared I'd have to prove it to Jeff, or anyone else who might think so. "Okay, I'm going to show you the picture of a cuckoo bird. You're not a cuckoo bird, this is…" I point at the bird for him.

Kiki's eyes focus intently on the photo. But he was bluffing. Waiting for me to buy into all this nonsense. He wanted to be an eagle. And nothing else.

Still, I'd play along. "See, you look nothing like that."

Kiki looked away momentarily with disbelieving eyes. "Why not?" If I'd insisted he couldn't be an eagle, he'd insist he could be anything he chose to be.

He wasn't making this easy on me. "This bird has a white stomach. And gray? You're gray. Sometimes you're just…" *Who we are born to be.* But I wouldn't say it. I couldn't hurt Kiki like that.

Couldn't tell him that sometimes in life we don't end up being what we aspire to become. That sometimes when we go off course, it's The Lord just putting us where we were meant to be.

Fighting me every step of the way, Kiki stands taller on his perch. Trying to be as tall as the bird in the photo, it'll never work. "Look. See?"

"I know. Okay." What to do? What to do? With Kiki trying so hard, my heart went out to him. Still, it was time to just blurt out the truth. "No matter how tall you stand—you're not going to be that big." There, I'd said it.

"Miracles happen, right?"

The bird trying to force me to be wrong, what Kiki needed was a reality check. And now. "It's not going to happen."

"Me becoming an eagle? My wings, they're longer every day."

"You can try. You can stretch every day as much as you want. But..."

"Some dreams can come true."

"It won't work." I hated having to be the heavy here. But I wouldn't let Kiki know I knew what he was trying to get at. "I hate to break the bad news to you. But you're not going to be a cuckoo bird. They're like fourteen inches long." I think about the bird in the photo in question. "This is huge."

"You saw how tall I am."

"You're tall." I was lying. Kiki wasn't that tall, even when he'd stood up and transformed himself. Though he didn't even have the entire use of his legs yet, usually folded in half like they were, he'd never be any taller than a grackle. "Wings too. Your wings look..." They looked downright weak still.

"I've been doing wing presses every day." And this wasn't a lie. While hanging onto his perch, he did beat his wings as hard as he could.

Flying frantically in place, he'd never once reached liftoff.

"I know you've been working on them. And they look really good." I so hoped he believed me. His wings were in fact looking better. His butt nub though? Nothing there yet to speak of. And a bird needed a tail to fly.

"I could be big as an eagle. I've been trying really hard to bulk up lately. All those meal worms."

"I know you have. But..."

"See?" He itches one of his wings with his teensy little talons. "I even have growing pains."

I paused to commiserate, but itches aren't growing pains. "All right, that one itches." I laugh at his inability to actually lie.

"Show me another picture then. So…"

"And did you want to see the picture of the eagle again?"

He didn't answer me, probably thinking I'd given in way too easy.

"Did you?" I knew darn well he wanted to see the eagle again. "You want to see the picture of the eagle?"

"I get it, Mom. You're out to prove to me I'm not an eagle."

"Because I think you should give up on the whole eagle…"

"Then I'll be one of those big parking lot birds."

"No, you're not a sea gull. That's really off the beaten path. We're nowhere near water."

The bird shrugs. "There's no oceans around here?"

Kiki was getting on my nerves now. A real first. "You're right in the middle of the country. There's no water here."

"I bet there's lakes though. Ponds. Creeks. Rivers."

Not about to let him trip me up, now pretending he could be a shore bird—I blather on. "You can—you don't even swim. You have to have those funny feet with the paddles between your feet. You don't have that. You got like, straight skinny little black feet. And you're not going to do well in water."

"Just turn to the pictures of the water fowl then."

"I mean, you want to look at the ducks?"

"Those black and white ducks."

Now he was really pulling my chain. "Penguins? You're definitely not a penguin. You got to be way up north in polar land to be a penguin. I'm thinking, all right…"

A grackle.

He cuts me off before I can say it. "A robin then?"

"Oooo. An American robin." I'm giddy now. Progress. At least we got back into the songbird category finally. "Oooh ha hoo." I hold the book closer to his beak. "Did you see this one?"

"I did. It could be my mother. I'm so excited."

And he's lying through his beak.

I talk to Jeff instead. "Aw, now tomorrow, that's all I'm gonna hear. American robin. Robin this. Robin that. He's gonna want to be a robin all day tomorrow now because of..." Because of nothing. It's all a smokescreen used to deflect his real intention of becoming an eagle. "He's going to have dreams about robins." I can say this like it's a fact.

But Kiki will only dream about becoming an eagle.

As I look with great intensity at the robin's orange chest, Kiki's not paying attention.

"She not my mother."

We'd made no progress at all here. The thrown confetti of reality will never come together for Kiki. "Did your mom look like this? No?"

Kiki suddenly refused to say a thing.

I'd gone on to pressure him for a yes. "No?"

The hurt, angry look was unmistakable. The glare. "You know what I am. An eagle."

Time to backpedal. The bird on to me, it felt awful to be in trouble with him. "I didn't in—I didn't intimate anything. What do you mean?" Having played innocent wouldn't get me far. "What?"

"Mom, just stop. I'm not a robin. I don't even have a red stomach."

Kiki intimated I was just being mean. "I know you don't have a red stomach. I'm not trying to be mean." I could never be mean to somebody who weighed no more than a single ounce.

"Me being an eagle, is that funny to you?"

"I'm not—I wasn't being funny." Things getting tense here, when the bird finally tried to break the ice with a nervous giggle, I'd laughed too. "Whaaaat?" Guilty as charged, the release felt good. Time to lie. "I was, I'm just trying to—okay. All right. Maybe I was being funny. All right. You can call it when you see it, man. You can."

"You think?"

"You can."

"But still—I'm an eagle. You'll see. When I'm gone for good, you'll know."

Gone for good.

The words tore into me. "I'm sorry." The guilt immense, the conversation having taken a turn back to seriousness, I must apologize. I'd tried to change a gift the good Lord gave me. And the sting of that felt awful.

"I'm sorry. I won't do it again." Say he's not an eagle. "Okay, we'll be serious. We'll be serious about this now." The abandoned bird having lost touch with his mother, it's not exactly something to be taken lightly.

Kiki looked tired again, sticking up for his dreams not easy.

"Okay, we're going to be serious. And we're going to look at..."

Kiki looked away. "Eagles?"

I'd thumbed through the book desperate to patch things up between us. Acting overly enthused about everything, it wouldn't fool him. "Oooh." I show Kiki a bird's photo I'd randomly come across.

Kiki's gray eyes darken at the sight. "Wait. Wait one second. I think I remember something."

"An olive sided fly catcher? Does that look familiar?"

Kiki stands taller on the perch, eyeing the photo closely. "Nope. Not an olive sided fly catcher. Sure of it as the beak on my face."

"This was a…"

Kiki had cut off my words. "Accident?" Bringing out the bird mug shots? The pink skin on his face having blushed, he seems resolute enough. "My eagle mother abandoned me. I just can't prove it yet."

"No way." He couldn't be sure of such a thing. "All right, now you're the one being funny. You're pulling my leg."

Kiki, trying to hold it together on the fumes of memory, is the one to give in this time around. "Mom was an olive sided fly catcher, all right."

But as soon as he'd admitted this, I wish I hadn't pushed him to give up on his dream. "Good one. An olive sided flycatcher." I can barely catch my breath, wondering how to backtrack on this mess. "You couldn't be funnier. You couldn't be. Good one."

"Can we stop it now?"

"All right." Like any decent mother, I lift his syringe, loaded with food and ready to go. Food always a good way to patch things up. "Let's eat and go to sleep again." I wave the tip in his face to see if he's hungry. "You want to?" He looks up at my hand. "Come on." He doesn't bite. "Come on. Do you want…"

"To eat? No."

"No?" I'd done it now. Kiki had never refused food before. "I'm not looking at this book anymore. I have a bug book."

No response.

"I have a bug book. There's like spiders in it and stuff. If you want to look at the bug book for a while..."

Nothing.

"I got flowers." I had a wildflower book to change the subject.

Kiki had only looked away in effort to show his disinterest. If he wanted to see anything, it would be pictures of eagles flying.

"Here." Giving up getting his mind off topic, I open the Audubon book to yet another page.

"That's her!" Kiki focused intently on all the photo's blue sky. On the huge black birds soaring through each and every fame—their wings spread wide. "That's my egg mother. An eagle."

Looking over the book from my upside down vantage point, none of these birds were actually eagles. But I wouldn't let Kiki in on my suspicions. A bird confused about his origins, I'd remain upbeat for his sake.

I'd let out a scary, "Oooo. Look at that. Wow. Look it. They're flying. Okay!"

Kiki, still unable to fly himself, seemed glum on his makeshift perch. Thinking I'd cheer him up, I'd turned the pages until I'd found some ducks. Adding sound effects he'd never heard before, ducks sure seemed funny.

"Quack, quack. Quack, quack."

The bird seemed ready to throw in the towel on his being an eagle fantasy. "What's is this bird?"

"Duck."

He'd taken the suggestion literally. "Why? Is something going to hit us?"

I force the issue playfully. Cringing. Ducking down for one falsely worried second. But with the baby looking even more forlorn, I'd felt compelled to tell the truth. "I didn't mean it literally."

"Then why did you do it? Duck."

"I did not mean it literally. Okay, it's a figure of speech, maybe."

"But you ducked."

I shake this all off, ready to move on to some other suggestion. "Maybe it's a bird thing." Turning the page, yet more ducks to look at, I'm happy there's no pictures of eagles here. I quack again. "Quack, quack, quack." I then repeat myself like a loon because Kiki thinks the sound is funny.

Turning the page again, Kiki gets bored. "More ducks?"

I checked the page, having to agree with him. "Wow, there's a lot of ducks in the world. What the heck?" I keep turning pages, sucking in air at the impressive sight we'd just run across. "Look at that!"

"It's not an eagle." The little bird stood up taller on his perch, checking out the giant white bird. He'd looked back at Jeff for a moment, making sure he'd seen this monster bird too. "What is it?"

Having forgotten the name of this bird, I sit stumped. "I don't even know what that is."

As I check the words written beneath the giant bird's photo, Kiki again turns to Jeff.

"It's a white pelican. With an orange..."

"Beak." That said, Kiki had sat back down on his haunches. Pointing to the huge water fowl with his own beak, he didn't trust my motivations. "You're saying I'm a pelican?"

"No, you don't look..."

73

He'd nodded. "Like a pelican? Because I'm not one. And look at that picture right there."

"This one?"

The miniature grayish bird had opened his beak. "That one."

"A swan? Are you a swan?" I can't help but laugh out the words.

"You know what I am."

I'd push this on him for a while. Would being a swan be any more ridiculous than insisting he's an eagle? "Are you going to turn into a swan?"

Kiki remained quiet.

"A trumpet swan?" Looking back at the page, I saw something else here I might suggest for him to be. "What are these?"

"I don't care."

"A whistling swan?" Was this any dumber than thinking he was an eagle? "I heard you whistle. You could be a whistling swan. I heard you whistle. Um…"

Kiki eyed the picture of some other bird there, egging me on.

"A mute swan? No, that's definitely not you. 'Cause you talk a lot."

"You talk more."

He'd had me there. "Well, okay, maybe not as much as me. True. But you do. You talk a lot."

"I'm not a stupid swan."

I'd push till he played along. "Okay, so you want to be a swan? Swans are nice."

"Let's just, I don't know, move on."

"All right." I guess we'd worn out the whole swan thing. Turning the page yet again, I had no idea what we'll find. "We have, oooo a grebe!"

His head turning towards the photo, he'd shivered. "Ick."

"Their weird looking. Grebes are like zombies. They got red eyes. Grebes, whoo! Grebes aren't happening."

"Turn the page. Quick!"

"Grebes aren't happening. No! No grebes. We're going to have nightmares tonight. Ugh!" Then I makes things worse by turning the page to an even bigger threat.

Kiki's neck had sunk down. Becoming frightened by what he saw, this time his transformer self got small. Not big. "Those eyes! They're worse!"

Holding the book open, I feign a frightened sound, the vacant deadly eyes of an owl before us. "An owl. A barred owl. Look at his eyes. Aren't they scary?"

"Shark eyes."

"Yeah. Oooo. Okay." Afraid the baby bird would have a heart attack, my own fluttering in my chest, I quickly get off this page. Goldfinches suddenly before us, this is as good a suggestion as any. "Those are pretty. These are real pretty."

"But they're yellow."

"Yeah. They're yellow. That's definitely not you. You're not yellow and…" I have no more suggestions, tired myself of this game. "Okay. I think we've seen enough."

Kiki's eyes misted up like they always had when he was about to say something to make me feel better. "I had a great time."

I'd smiled at how caring he could be. A homeless waif. No real memories of his mother—his father—to make him feel whole.

I look back at him. "It was fun." Turning the pages randomly, I'd been more than ready to close the book on this little escapade. "We have a lot to dream about tonight. We can dream about all these birds."

Having cocked his head at a certain picture of a tiny wren, he was getting sleepy. "Those aren't my parents either."

No, they weren't. They weren't because Kiki was probably a grackle. A common grackle. But that was one thing he would never admit.

Looking down at Kiki, he was already bigger than these birds. "Those are the little teeny ones. Okay, goodnight."

Being only mid afternoon, he'd sleep and dream about all that we'd seen until waking up for his next feeding. So, closing the bird mug shot book, I quietly got up from my chair, pretending to leave.

Staying close by, I'd waited until his eyes closed. Turning his head and tucking it under a wing, he was soon sound asleep. And when he was, I'd carefully picked up his whole entire perch. Placed inside his cat carrier where he'd be safest, I fastened the door shut good and tight.

Looking wistfully out the window, I'd wondered if this excursion had helped or not. I wondered if Kiki would ever get over the hurtful notion that his real mother had been a great and beautiful bald eagle. Because even if Kiki had been an eagle, I couldn't possibly love him any more than I already did. In fact, being the plain little bird that he was made me love him all the harder.

It was only later that I'd found out that Kiki and Jeff had shared an inside joke at my expense this day. That being how the grocery bag I'd used for random doodle hits was hooked on the doorknob behind my chair.

You haven't lived until you've been made the vent of jokes by a baby wild bird.

CHAPTER 6 (VIDEO 6)
THE WORLD BEYOND

June 5, early morning

When Kiki was about two weeks old, he'd wanted to go outside all by himself. To fly. To try out his wings. He'd related all this while his miniature blackbird feet curled themselves tightly around a curtain rod. Teetering there, he'd daydreamed the minutes away.

Having seen a flock of blue jays fly down into a tree outside, he'd made a quick comparison. Looking down over his own scrawny body, he was crestfallen. Still a complete mess of opening pin feathers and baby down, the truth was all too apparent.

He was still too young to fly.

Sadly, he'd have to remain grounded today. But that fact didn't stop him from dreaming of flying effortlessly one day soon. Of flying like those blue jays, now dotting the massive blue spruce out back like stained glass windows.

Kiki's wings tips slumping at the thought, he knew only one thing. That his days of gaining their phenomenal aerial stunt work were far ahead of him.

Standing at the little bird's side, both of us looked wistfully out over the back yard. But honestly, the area at the back of the house wasn't a back yard at all. Because the house sat on the high ridge of a valley, from this vantage point, you'd think you were far up in a tree house.

Or you could've been a bird standing on the uppermost branches of a tree.

The treetops swaying in the warm breeze were so thick, the view of the undulating corn fields beyond would stay obliterated all summer long.

There was no way I'd ever allow Kiki to venture outside alone yet. No real nest to call his own, unable to feed himself yet, I felt guilty I couldn't spend every waking second at his side like this. Real mother birds didn't have houses to sell—like I did. Houses that needed to be cleaned for the ever intrusive showings that kept popping up. The showings I'd resented because they took me away from Kiki.

And so, wanting Kiki to live a long happy life, I couldn't very well stick him outside. All alone. In a cage at this tender age. Not with weasels waiting out there to get him. Not with the ever present hungry raccoons foraging the woods we'd now looked out upon.

Not with the sharp shinned hawk—and eagles—I'd seen blow over the house on occasion.

Instead, here we'd stood, Kiki and I. At this window. Happy at least for this one cherished moment in time that we could remember always. Looking out the window with him and through the trees, I saw him in my mind's eye, happily soaring over the woods out back.

"Just think, Kiki. Someday. All of this will be yours."

And it would be. That is, if I could get the little bird healthy enough to release one fine day. If I could get him from this point to that—alive. If I'd made no disastrous mistakes along the way to impede his progress. To hurt him. So much could go wrong.

And then there'd be the release itself. Acid churned in my stomach thinking about it. Thinking about the courage it would take.

Letting my beloved Kiki go would be like having love in the palm of your hand fly off for forever.

After many silent moments, emotions rose in Kiki about the immense woods before him too. But his were all positive, not one to back down to a challenge. "Now! Now! Now!"

Glad a pane of glass stood before the bird and the great outdoors, I hated to be the bearer of bad news. That he'd have to know how to fly first.

Exasperated at the thought of so many acres of forest to fly through, the infant bird felt horribly penned in. But, he'd at least decided to get ready for the event. Attempting to pull the last of the sheaths off its feathers, he could in this way prepare for his big day.

Later that day, I got Kiki to take a sip of water out of a Dixie cup all by himself. A real milestone in his development, I decided to give him some breathing room at the front of the house for a change. Standing him up on yet another curtain rod, he was now in yet another bedroom. And a whole different world beaconed to him from this new vantage point. Eying the bird bath and feeders, he'd watched all the other flying life forms in the yard. Birds he may one day come to meet.

As I stood silently watching from the doorway, Kiki daydreamed about how life was going so far.

Thinking about his progress—at how he could now drink all by himself, he felt ready for the challenges of the world. But he also knew he wasn't even a full fledged fledgling yet. He could only sit there and watch the cars go by on the street. The milk trucks. All the Mad Max farm machinery. The mailman's car—which had scared him.

The jeep being the only vehicle to stop at the box by the street, it was frightening.

This other world opening strangely before Kiki, it seemed a dangerous world. And I was glad he mulling over all the good tips I'd been giving him lately.

Don't fly into a window pane.

Don't land on any unsuspecting stranger's head.

Don't talk with your beak full.

Don't cross the street—either by flying or walking.

Sure, the low flying birds who kamikazied the road were usually females, eggs weighing them down, but these were just tips. Dumb tips. I was a joke. His real mother would've been much more useful. She would eventually show him where to find bugs. And water. And which berries would be safe to eat. She'd know how to keep the cruel world at bay too. A world full of predators.

Predators waiting to collide with his innocence at release time. Say, the eagle flock he'd intended to one day join at his own peril.

Worried out of my mind that I was a woefully deficient mother, I dreaded the day we'd have to say goodbye. But for now, we at least still had this day. A day to be shared in the same house. A day to still be together. But these days were woefully numbered. And that fact had grated on me each time I'd awoken to feed him in the middle of the night. Little wonder it took hours for me to fall back asleep.

Kiki looked small, standing in the window on his curtain rod perch. So small and helpless, the world looming ever larger before him.

CHAPTER 7 (VIDEO 7)
KIKI FINDS HIS MAGIC

June 5, late morning
Ever since Kiki had jumped headlong into the vase of roses on my
desk, he'd been itching to fly for real. Thought he'd thought he was
ready for his first flying lesson, he wasn't even fully feathered yet.
I'd been sure he'd take off with blind enthusiasm.

Only to crash land on the floor.

Having no idea how a mother bird arrives at this point, the
actual teaching of flight, I had no idea how to proceed either.

I'd only gotten over my own fear of flying myself in the past
few years. I'd always avoided jets and hot air balloons and
helicopters like the plague. But I hadn't been the type of person
who'd allowed myself the luxury of fear. And neither was this baby
bird.

Thankfully, only a few years ago, I'd flown like a bird myself.
Or as close to it as a human can get. Yes, I'd go up there. In all the
wind. With nothing between me and the ground but a great, blue
nothingness.

Yes, I'd taken a free flying lesson on a fixed wing ultra-light.

Stomach in knots, I'd taken off one hot summer day—like Kiki
would today. Though I'd had the big shock of finding out how darn
cold it had been a thousand feet up in the air—Kiki would be flying
in my bedroom. The instructor even allowing me to land the craft, I
remember how my arms shook, struggling to keep the control bar

steady. Having landed safely, he'd then told me the biggest secret of flying.

That most crashes happen when landing.

That said, I'd been a big stickler on getting this fact across to Kiki. The bird having fidgeted on his perch at the table, I couldn't tell if he'd been eager to accomplish flight.

Or scared to try it for the very first time.

I sat in my chair before him. As the sun blazed in through the windows, I looked down at the bird. If my knee caps were shaking, his must've been worse. Jeff having entered the room with his camera rolling, we were ready to begin.

"So I'm here with Kiki. Who has a new book coming out. Kiki and The Bird Whisperer." I shook his feeding syringe before his beak, hoping he'd take a hit to slake his nerves. "Kiki and The Bird Whisperer, and—what?" I'd stopped talking, Kiki having interrupted me.

"Kiki and soon to be..." He'd stopped there, obviously tossing around different concepts in his head.

I'd pressed him to finish his thought. "Kiki and soon to...what?"

He'd suddenly opened his wings, the joy boundless. "Kiki, Soon To Be A Major Motion Picture."

I repeated the title pensively. "Kiki, Soon To Be A Major Motion Picture."

No way. I waved his feeding syringe before his face nervously. This would never fly with the booksellers. You weren't supposed to use a title that was misleading. And this title was big time misleading. I'd keep the original book's title without telling him.

"And today we're going to..." Not this again. "What?" I won't do it, say this for him.

He lets loose a blood curdling squawk.

"Okay, today he wanted me to remind everyone that his father was an eagle." Rolling my eyes, whereas I so wished he would give this idea up, I also wished it could be true for his sake.

"Say it again."

"Okay. His father was an eagle." I wave the tube, hoping he'll eat. He'll need his strength for this first try at going airborne. "And um…"

"I can't eat. I'm too excited."

I'd tried to coax him to anyway. "Come on, come on, Kik." I tried all the usual tricks to get him to open his beak. Saying his name usually worked. So that's what I tried first. "Kik! Kik!" Nothing. "Let's go Kik! Let's go!"

"Can't. If I eat, I'll weight more."

"Okay." I'd put down the syringe, hoping he knew more about flight that I knew. "All right. So today…"

Dear God, this can't be happening—the flying lesson.

"Today…" I start again, trying to say what we're about to do—fly. But if the thought gave me cotton mouth, how dry would Kiki's be? Out to buy time before the big event, I'd picked up the plastic cup of water. I'd held it to the tip of his beak, hoping he'd take a sip. "Let's see if he wants to drink some water. Kik? Water?"

The agitated baby bird looks off to Jeff. "Water. At a time like this? Let's fly!"

I move the cup away with a shaking hand. What if he crashes down to the floor? Flies into the mirror? Hits the wall? He'll get hurt. "No? Okay." Taking a sip myself, I put down the glass with dread, hoping something gets in the way to stop our first attempt at flight. "All right. Today we're…"

Now it was Kiki's turn to get cold feet—er, wing. The bird having turned away from me.

"I thought we're going to fly today?"

"My wings—they're not eagle wings."

With a pensive smile, I won't let him back out of something he'd wanted to try so badly. Finishing my introduction on what's about to take place, I'd given him some time to mentally prepare.

"Today we're going to have our first flight lesson. And, oh!" The integral moment had been interrupted.

A doodle softly slapping the paper beneath Kiki's perch, I'd at first thought his nerves had gotten the better of him. Then the truth dawned on me all at once. He'd done it in order to weigh less. Baby bird droppings that much more bulky than an adults.

Kiki having known this intuitively had stunned me. Comparatively, humans didn't seem born with any instincts at all anymore.

"All right. Good thing to do that before flying. Because it, it lightens the load." After chuckling nervously, the smile is genuine. I love Kiki's eyes. The way they move when following me. "That was good. That was perfect. See now, that's something I really wouldn't have known to do at the first flight. But that was really good."

Being a mother bird to Kiki, it seemed I had nothing of real value by way of tips to offer him.   Trying regardless to be of help to him, I'd stumble on through—learning from *him* as I went.

Having put my finger before his feet, Kiki tripped getting up onto it. "I'm scared to fly, I think." Flapping his wings to right himself, his toes shook against my finger.

With him being frightened, the worry rose fresh in me. "So now we're going to attempt flight." This said, the time here—butterflies rose in my stomach.

What if he flew into the wall? The closet door? The windows high up in the house's peak—fourteen feet high? He could break his neck. A wing. His breastbone.

"Is it time?" Then Kiki clung harder with his little feet. He'd hunkered down. His wings flapped in hot anticipation. "Is it really time?"

I looked him over, this minute being made of feathers and hollow bones. And, Dear God, he still had no tail feathers to speak of. They weren't even a half inch long yet. Were we crazy to have attempted such a thing so early?

Kiki folded his wings down and looked me in right in the face. "Wait!" He'd gotten cold feet at the last possible moment. "I'm not so sure about this anymore."

Time for a pep talk, I held the bird up to my face. Trying to calm myself my voice rose disturbingly anyway—equally as worried as the bird. "Now, it's exactly like I told you. Don't forget. It's the landings. It's the landings. It's all in the landings. Are we ready?"

"Okay." Kiki had gotten up his nerve at last, his toes loosening their grip. "So what do I do?"

No real advice to offer him, I was devastatingly out of my element. No wings to speak of to call my own, the hand he'd stood on was now trembling. Moving Kiki to my other hand, I did it in effort to acquire more airspace. But this position wouldn't do either. No, not at all.

No real last minute instructions to offer him, he was on his own from here on in. Nervously moving him into position back on my other hand, his wings flapped wildly. It was now or never.

"Mom, what do I do?"

I gulped and tried to act like I knew what I was doing. "Okay. Here, you're going to come onto this hand.

"What for?"

"Come on."

Being forced into this, he'd found his air legs. Suddenly standing tall, wings down, he was ready.

"Good boy, Kiki."

"Are you sure I'm a boy?"

Having called him a boy for a while now, I knew what he was up to here. The bird was stalling for time. And I'd give it to him.

"All right, Kik, whatever. We really don't know. We're having a gender identity problem here. Because, we don't know if Kik's a girl or a boy but—these things happen."

"I'm ready! I think."

"Okay, Kik." I laugh, remembering how it felt to jump into the deep end of the pool for the first time. "We're going to fly! You ready?"

I'd dropped my arm so he'd fly up off it.

Adding a soundtrack to the momentous event, I'd belted out Wagner's RIDE OF THE VALKYRIES. But Kiki only flew only inches. And stopped cold on my other hand.

His wings flapped furiously. "You used the wrong music!"

"What?" I lowered my arms in disbelief. I'd ruined everything. Just everything.

Kiki turned to face me down, total disgust written all over his face. "That wasn't *eagle* music."

Egg on my face, I had no idea what eagle music was. "I'm sorry. It was the wrong song."

"Use Darth Vader's theme."

I'd have to tell Jeff, waiting behind his camera. "Okay. Um, he wants the theme song from Darth Vadar."

Kiki, still standing on my hand, had grown excited. "Mom!"

Trying to remember the song, I took a second. "I can do that. I can do that. I'm sorry. I'm sorry. I didn't…" I'd gone on to stutter like I always do when flustered. "Uh, how, how would I know?" Taking in a deep breath, I begin singing the song.

But though Kiki's wings are flapping, he still has his toes curled around my finger. Hanging on for dear life, he was too scared to fly. But with the song gaining momentum—Kiki suddenly forgot his fear.

And jumped.

He flew through the air. He suspended time. His wings flapped in slow motion. It seemed he'd never get to his destination. Flying the span of a good twelve inches, space elongated before him. Then all at once, Kiki landed on top of his cat carrier. His feet—churning to grip at something.

And there he stood. Stunned. Out of breath. In shock.

I'm laughing like a fool. He's laughing like a fool. I'm clapping my hands. He's flapping his wings. And I'm so lost in the utter oblivion of mother bird joy, it's as if I'd flown myself.

Then the gushing starts. "Whoa ha, ha! Kik! Excellent work, Kik! Excellent work."

Kiki looking around the room, he's still stunned. "I did it! I flew! I flew!"

Jumping out of my chair, to hug him, I'd picked him up.

But he squirmed to get free. "I'm ready for outside!"

He'd eyed the window, ready to bound for it. Not knowing a pane of glass stood before him and freedom, he could yet kill himself.

Scooping him up quickly in my hands, I'd pressed his little body beneath my chin ever so lightly. "Good boy, Kik. Excellent work."

Not having corrected me on his gender this time, I think I may be correct in the assumption. "It's all in the thigh muscles."

Looking me straight in the eye, he'd wanted the truth. "Did I land like an eagle?"

"It was perfect. It was absolutely perfect."

Hugging Kiki to my cheek, I thought that surely, this is the best moment of my entire life. Here, with this little bird who'd stumbled so blindly into my heart. Him having proved to me again that the best things in life *are* indeed free.

Grinning impossibly at him, I babbled. "Good boy."

"Girl?"

This again. "Girl, Kik." The bird now held at my other cheek, I'm so out of my mind happy I think I'll bust. "Excellent work. Excellent work."

"I'm so happy!" Kiki still seemed stunned to have actually done it—flown. "Thanks, Mom. Thanks for making me believe I could do anything."

Sitting back down holding Kiki, this was truly a celebration. A celebration marking how unbelievably wonderful life can be with one of God's joyous little creatures. And I knew I'd never forget this blissful moment. It was just that overwhelming an experience.

Being privileged to share in the miracle of a baby bird's first flight, a true godsend.

CHAPTER 8 (VIDEO 8)
DOING THINGS TOGETHER

June 5, early afternoon

After Kiki's flying lesson, I'd fed him and sat him on my shoulder.
Ambling through the living room, we'd tiptoed past the dove's cage.
And all because they were frightened of any black bird that
happened to cruise outside their window. Crows, turkey vultures,
eagles. Even though Kiki was a measly fledgling, they'd make no
exception.

Cutting through the kitchen, we'd made our way down the
basement stairs. A walkout, we'd stopped before the set of sliding
glass patio doors. Having earlier set out a curtain rod specifically for
Kiki, I'd put his feet on it. Getting up onto my mini trampoline, I
was out to get some much needed exercise.

As I ran in place, Kiki worked on his leg muscles too. Doing
calisthenics by just sitting there, he stayed immobile. Both of us
peering outside at the forest beyond—we'd spent our days together.
Working. Dreaming.

And me shrinking from the day I'd have to let my best bud go.

Beyond our little world. Beyond the sliding glass doors.
Summer seemed to lie in wait for that ever dreaded moment. Every
second of every minute was that precious together. And I couldn't
fathom how I'd ever let this little bird go. Couldn't picture it in my
mind, how it would go. I just wasn't strong enough yet. And I didn't
think I ever would be.

Both our eyes watching the mulberry tree, the wind rustling its leaves enthralled us. We saw catbirds come and go, berries crushed in their beaks. Saw a squirrel there hanging upside down, filling itself full.

And as I peered past Kiki, I'd watched the tall forest that snaked down to the farming valley below. The corn there stilted from a drought, my mind wandered into fresh fields of worry. Kiki, perched silent but watchful, looked down into the valley too.

Lazy thoughts coursing slowly through both our heads, the worry of first flight was long behind us.

Enjoying each other's company, this mystery bird and me, that persistent thought came back to gnaw away at me. The cruel world waiting beyond this very glass, that same awful thought struck my heart harder than ever.

One day soon I'll have to release you.

Dear God, the thought alone was enough to kill me dead. Kiki remained upbeat though. All the sunshine. All the blue and green colors. It all masked how dark the world can be. And I ran on behind him, just wishing he'd never have to leave me behind.

On this little road to nowhere, going to a place I never wanted to get to, I ran on. Pained by the thought of us one day being separated, Kiki would need his freedom. A wild bird, it would be cruel to keep him caged his whole life long. But we at least had this.

This one moment together where all was yet well in this unforgiving world that was ours. Knowing I was soon to face the prospect of losing Kiki, I could not remember what my life had been like before he'd entered it.

And so, though losing him would mean I'd have my ordinary world back, I sure didn't want it much. This little journey we were both on, becoming the new normal for us—how would we ever say goodbye? How? How would I one day set him free?

Knowing he may never come back to me?

CHAPTER 9 (VIDEO 9)
HARP SONG

June 5, early evening

Not long thereafter, Kiki thought I should get a grip on the whole loss thing. Having noticed my harp in the living room corner, he wanted me to play. Its gold crown and feet standing in quiet majesty of the moment, I'd placed him upon my shoulder. Then I sat down.

The doves, unable to see his wild bird self from behind the harp, they could enjoy the concert too. My male dove, Lovey, usually bursting into song when I played.

But today, I was determined to find something special to play for Kiki—my little gift from God. Then, turning the pages of my book of hymns, I'd found the perfect song.

Just as I'd taken a seat behind the strings, Kiki hunkered down, making himself comfortable on my shoulder. "A concert, Mom. For me?" He stared forward at the notes on the staves, wondering what it all meant.

Quietly waiting for me to begin, I'd raised my arms and put my hands upon the strings. The tiny bird watched intently as I placed the fingers of my left hand on a low G chord. Arpeggiating the notes upwards for lavish effect, I'd then paused. Taking in a deep breath, I began to sing.

"Morning has broken." I didn't get very far before being interrupted.

My male dove, Lovey, having indeed broken into song with me. "Coo. Coo. Coo."

I smiled and somehow kept going. "Like the first morning. Blackbird has…"

"Eagles are black!" Kiki stood up excitedly. The song about blackbirds, he'd plunked right back down. "Keep going."

But I'd begun to laugh. Stopping the song, my head against my harp, I say the words too. "Blackbird has!"

"Keep going! Keep going!"

I'd managed somehow, singing again. "Spoken like the first bird."

Kiki's toes curled in, having slipped in a teensy question. "You're playing an eagle song. For me."

I'd ignored this outburst to spare his feelings. But I did smile at his hope, and sung on. "Praise for the singing"

Kiki moves closer to my face, his body having pressed against my cheek. "I love this song."

I had to hold back the giggles. "Praise for the morning. Praise for them springing fresh from the Word."

Hearing the last chord being arpeggiated upwards, Kiki had gotten bummed. "It can't be over. Not this soon."

I'd closed my eyes against being this in love with him and hit a few low notes.

Kiki couldn't contain himself. "I love you."

Turning my head towards him, he'd looked into my face. Unable to quell the emotions, I'd answered him. "I love you." My throat constricts with emotion, the second one coming out high and squeaky. "Love you. Love you." About to cry, I'd fought it with everything I had.

Kiki moved instinctively backwards on my shoulder, not wanting to see me cry. "Don't."

"Come here, sweetie." I'd placed the harp's front feet back on the floor to free up my hands. Then I'd reached around for him with both of them. "Come here, baby." Setting him on my finger, I'd then begun to sing *a cappella*—unaccompanied—and right into his ear. "Blackbird has spoken, like the first bird."

Holding his beak in the air, he'd looked right into my eyes. "Am I that bird?"

"That's you." I'd nuzzled my nose against his beak. "That's you. That's you. That's you."

"Don't stop."

Knowing I couldn't take much more, I kept singing regardless. I sang because I couldn't help myself. Rocking my baby to and fro on the cradle of a single finger, I'd cherish this moment forever.

"Blackbird has spoken, like the first bird." Lovey joining in again, we'd both sung to Kiki. "Praise for them singing..." I'd started to laugh again—Kiki having tapped my nose with his beak.

"I sing too." But he'd sang only when the vacuum cleaner was on to hide his practicing beneath other sounds.

"Praise for the morning, praise for them springing, fresh from the Word."

Lost in the moment, Kiki had wanted more. Not knowing what another round could unleash. "Sing it again, the song?"

My lips had touched his face ever so lightly, the kiss barely having registered with him. "Morning has broken, like the first morning, blackbird has spoken like the first bird, praise for the singing, praise for the morning, praise for them springing fresh from the Word."

After that last note, I'd kissed Kiki on his chest. And, having rested my forehead against his cheek, I'd used this moment to compose myself. It didn't work.

I'd looked up at Jeff, in the doorway, filming us again. And, with the floodgates threatening to open, I'd finally admitted it to my husband. The truth.

"I'm gonna, I'm going to lose him someday." I'd laughed in order to stop the dam from bursting. "I'm going to lose him someday." The tears had been right there. Surfacing, ready to fall. My face going red, trying my hardest to bite them back, I just kept repeating that awful thought. "I don't want to." I'd hidden my face behind Kiki's body. But it was too small to hide behind. "I don't want to." Looking down, I'd started to cry. Hard.

"Don't. Or I'll cry too." Kiki's heart taking a hit right along with mine, he didn't know what to do either.

Trying to compose myself for the baby bird's sake, my head pounding, I just couldn't do it. So we both got up and left the room. To cry together. In private.

And there'd been no mistaking it. I'd already lost part of my heart to him. I'd lost it the moment he looked out from his carrier when we'd first met. And though neither of us would ever be same, there was no going back now. We loved each other, Kiki and I.

And if the world ended tomorrow, we would at least have this one song to remember each other by. A song about a lowly, little black bird.

One of the *least* of these has filled my heart the most.

CHAPTER 10 (VIDEO 10)
DOODLE CATASTROPHE

June 8, sometime after noon

Kiki had graduated up to living in a huge cage in my bedroom. It was three feet long by two feet wide. Learning to fly from branch to branch, it was really more of a hop-fly. One done with great uncertainty at that.

Flying pretty good between the branches set at each end, I'd gotten him to fly back and forth. I did so by enticing him with treats of meal worms and fresh mulberries.

But I had an even better surprise for him today.

A surprise that would take place beneath the big blue yonder. What with me having put on my camouflaged skirt and yellow tank top, it should've been the tipoff we'd be going outside.

Placing the little fledgy inside his cat carrier for the trek outside, he had no idea where we'd be going. He'd travelled well though. Locked behind the metal grill of his door, he didn't even go nuts. Or fly all over the place. This beautiful summer day, bound to be one full of momentous surprises—I had no idea just how shocking they'd be.

For both Kiki—and me.

And for more reasons than one, as it turned out.

The sun, high overhead, it lit the occasion like a heavenly spotlight. For the first time ever, Kiki would enjoy a modicum of freedom. It was the first time he'd be able to fly from one big tree branch to another. Because I'd wedged one in each corner of his brand spanking new flight cage. I'd also had Jeff jam one high up in its peak.

Though he'd put it too high up for me to reach.

Standing beneath it, safely zipped up inside the flight cage's screened in walls, I'd opened Kiki's carrier. Taking him out of it, I thought he'd fly for the tree branches. But he didn't. Instead, he'd hung on to my finger for dear life. Loud vehicles zooming past on the street, I could feel his fear. Feel his teensy little knees going all jittery. Plowing on for his sake, I knew he'd come around. This much freedom being almost more nerve wracking then first flight, I was sure he'd fly from branch to branch here.

I'd looked off to Jeff, locked inside the cage right along with, camera in tow. "Hi. Today Kiki and I are in our high tech flight cage."

Kiki, standing on my finger, the one held before my face, turned and glared my way. "It's not really a flight cage."

Found out, the smile had instantly dropped from my face. With the camera rolling, I'd have to act all innocent. Surely, the bird would drop the subject if I played dumb. "What?"

"Tell the truth."

Sucking in my ego, I smile to smooth things over. "Okay. It's a Coleman picnic tent." I thought for sure I'd seen the bird smiling, proud of me. "God's creature's don't have the ability to lie, I guess." I was so proud of Kiki's ethics, I'd broken into quite the revival song, my soul singing. "Alleluia. Alleluia. Alleluuuuuia."

Kiki turned to me, the anticipation mounting. "Now what?"

I'd have to break the news to him why we'd come out here. But the thought had scared me so much. Him flying. Outside. To branches set about eight feet apart. Little wonder I hadn't told him what we'd be attempting out here in the yard.

And then I said it. "So. We're going to attempt flight today. This is the first time."

"Outside!" The bird's voice had cracked, busting with anticipation. I so hoped he wouldn't just rush into this. "And, um. I just wanted…" The big moment upon us, the worry mounting, so many last minute details needing to be checked. "I need to know if you, if your ailerons are in the right place. And you got to remember to keep your gears up."

"Roger that. Gears up."

"Okay, keep your gears up. And we're gonna…" I thought my heart would give out. What if Kiki crashed to the ground and broke a wing? It would be my fault for pushing this on his too soon. "Just remember everything I told you about landing." And right here, Kiki had stopped me cold.

Trying vehemently to get my attention, he'd used his hardest hitting bird sound. "CHUCK!"

"What?"

"What if my feathers aren't long enough? My tail? You keep stressing that it's all in the landing."

I'd listened to his complaint with profound compassion. But felt I'd been right too. "It's still the thing. I'm sorry. I—you think it's not? You, you think it's the wings?"

"Yeah, I think it's the wings." He looked outside the screened wall and up at the sky. Big and blue and endless overhead. "You try flying. Go ahead. I'll watch."

That shut me up good. "All right. Well, work on the wings then. Work on the—all right." I so feared he'd hurt himself. "We're both right." I wink weakly. "Work on the wings. And, uh, tell me how it goes when you get there."

Kiki stood high on my finger, his skinny legs stretching up for height. His grip loosening, he looked forward, pure concentration ripping across his face. "I'm ready."

Having held my hand before his body so he wouldn't lift off too soon, I'd lowered it. Saying the magic words, I look forward in anticipation of lift off. "On your mark. Get set. Go!"

Flinging my hand forward towards the propped up branch in the corner, his little wings flapping madly. But Kiki's grip on my hand had tightened—just as it had for the flying lesson in my room. Still sitting on my finger, something's gone terribly wrong. Again.

He'd chucked loudly again. "I'd lost my nerve."

"You're scared." I reeled in my hand, having held it before my heart. Secretly glad he didn't attempt this, butterflies raged inside my stomach. "I understand this." Glossing over the snafu for his sake, I had to think something up to cover for him. And quick. "Did you clear it with the tower?"

"What tower?" Kiki looked around the yard, no tower in sight.

"Oh, oh, okay. Then that was the problem." With Kiki looking down at his feet, I gave further instructions. "Clear it with the tower."

"Done."

"Okay. Clear for takeoff! Clear for takeoff for Kiki!" I could tell he didn't want to do this, try this again. So I'd cajoled him into it. "Clear for takeoff!"

Regardless of all my excitement, the bird had just stood on my finger. Immobile. Not even one wing flapped this time. "The branch, it's too far away. I'm a failure as a bird."

I smiled at him. "Okay." And though the fissure in my own heart had widened for his sake, I had to make light of the situation. Maybe Kiki was taking this all too seriously. So I broke the ice by laughing. "Kik. It's like I told you. You can do this. I know that…"

"You don't know the first thing about flying."

He had me there, the serious again mounting within me. "All right. Let's try this."

Kiki mumbles something under his breath. Something about an eagle, of course.

"What?" I ask him.

"You forgot, Mom. Again."

"All right. I'm sorry." And once again, it appeared the problem had been with me. Not him. "I forgot. I, it wasn't my fault. I can't remember everything." I'd try harder, the egg on my face building up there. "Okay. The eagle is going to take off." Behind his back, I ask Jeff to go along with me for his sake. "The eagle is going to take flight. It's the first time ever. *Outside*."

Kiki had hunkered down. This time, he seemed ready to fly to the branch. The width, to him, looking wider than the Grand Canyon.

I cajole him on. "The eagle is going to take flight." Outstretching my hand, he'd stunned me.

Suddenly gone—Kiki was airborne with a loud exhilarating, "Chirp!"

Barreling across the flight cage, the baby bird had gone all of four feet from hand to branch. But he'd landed successfully.

Grabbing the branch that teetered against the screen wall, he was quite out of breath. "I did it! I flew! FAR!"

"Yes!" Racing over to Kiki, I'd clapped as I went. "The eagle has landed! The eagle has landed!" I wanted nothing to ruin his big moment, saying under my breath to Jeff, "Just go along with me here."

Lifting Kiki in my hand, he'd looked outside the tented area. Looked at all the freedom out there for the taking. "Someday, right?"

"Good boy, Kiki."

"Boy." He squawks in possible protest. "What if I'm not?"

"Girl." I'd corrected myself. This again. "Good Kiki." And then all the gushing had begun as I'd rubbed him into my forehead. As I'd hugged his tiny, weightless body under my chin. "You're my baby."

He'd looked away, red faced. "Uh, Mom?"

"Kik!" I'd remained oblivious to his embarrassment.

Getting the full glare again, his eyes are on me. "Stop it!"

"What?" Stunned, my heart stalling out, something's changed between us with his newfound freedom. "Don't say that anymore? In public?"

"I'm an eagle." He'd felt older now. More accomplished.

"Okay. Kik's an eagle," I admit. And I forgive him for having grown up so quickly. My heart singing with laughter for him. "Kik's an eagle."

He chirps loudly. "I'm an eagle."

Then, though safely tucked behind our screen wall, the sound of a big truck ripped by. Going a frightening sixty miles an hour, I thought back to the crow released at the wildlife center. The one hit by the car. If the screen wall hadn't been here—might that have happened to Kiki?

Looking down at Kiki, all his eagle bravado had vaporized into thin air. He'd once again turned back into being a fledgling bird.

I'm stuttering again, wondering what to do. "Oh, oh. Oh, boy."

"What was that?" Kiki asks, thrown headlong back into babydom.

"Oooo." Using this truck as a learning experience, maybe he'd stay away from them someday. "You're gonna see a lot of those. That's a milk truck. 'Cause we live by the cows."

"And you're saying I'm a cowbird?"

"You're not a cowbird. Remember?" Wanting him to know he'd really been a grackle, I wouldn't say it. "You're not…you're…okay. I know that you, uh." I had no idea how to fix this.

"Think I'm an eagle?"

Those accusatory, but sad eyes on me, I could just die. "I wasn't intimating anything."

His feelings were hurt. "Maybe it's you, Mom. Who can't identify a young eaglet."

"What? I wasn't…"

Again, he breaks eye contact with me, this time going so far as to turn his back on me. Which really hurt.

"Boy, you, you know? You're touchy today. I don't know why."

"Because out here—I need to be an eagle."

The problems between us mounting, I decide to defuse the problem with over the top comedy. "Because you're outside, you don't need Mom anymore?" Pretending to cry, I hope he'll play along. "Is that it?" I press my face toward him. 'Cause you're outside, you don't know Mom anymore?"

Not in the mood to play along, Kiki flew up into the tent's peak.

Up where I couldn't reach him, I could do nothing more than helplessly stand directly beneath him.

I was worried he'd fall. "Kik? Kik? Come down from there."

"No. It's too high. I'm scared."

The tension mounting, I'd wondered if I should go get a ladder from the garage. "Kiki! Kiki! Kik? Come on down, Kik." At this point, the worry had showed up in my voice. "Kik?"

Nothing.

"Come down, Kik." At this point, I'd irrationally thought I'd never see him again. Never hold him. Never feed him. "Kiki? Kik? Come on. You have to come down."

The fledgling bird wouldn't budge off the branch. A branch I couldn't reach.

I'd resorted to bribing to get him down. "We're going to eat or something. Come on. Kiki?"

And then it happened.

POOP!

I got gob smacked. With something hot. Right in the face.

Looking crossways, I could see a thick, whitish blob go sliding down the tip of my nose. Doodle sliding down onto my lips, I looked up at him, helplessly.

Kiki peered down at me. "It was an accident!"

"I love you anyway! I love you anyway!" Laughing till I was about to cry, I couldn't help but repeat myself, sliding a tissue from my skirt pocket. "Kik! Kiki! Oh!" Cleaning off my nose, my lips, I'd looked down into the tissue aghast. "Where'd he...? Ugh!"

Then, having heard the beating of baby angel wings, the worry ripped into joy. Kiki had come down safely. He'd landed on the branch next to me.

"There you are." My hands outstretched to the bird, all the tension melted when he'd jumped joyously onto my finger. And when he'd laid down upon it, my laughter was more than genuine.

"Mom, I'm sorry."

"Kik." Holding back the tears of joy, he had to know that some accidents could be forgiven. "I love you anyway." Time to move on. "You want to go in and eat?" I knew he had to be hungry, all this flying about being hard work.

He watched me clean off my face some more, with rapt eyes. "I'm still sorry." He had to let this thing go.

I looked at the bird. "You want to eat something?" Then I'd licked my lips. "Oh!" The taste was familiar. "Mulberries?"

Kiki looked away from me, mortified. "I'll never eat another mulberry."

Again, I'd make light of this to spare him the humiliation. "Uh huh. Okay. No more mulberries for you. And so, you want to go eat now?"

"Do we have to?"

"I have to go and wash my face."

"I hate myself."

He'd needed yet more encouragement. "I love you. I love you."

"But I had an accident." His toes tightened their grip on my finger. And he'd hunkered down lower still.

A pep talk was in order. "I know. I know. It worked out well today. You did a fabulous…"

He stood up slightly, all his attention focused on my opinion. "Did I look majestic?"

"Yes. You looked like an eagle when you were flying. You looked just…" I'd rubbed at my soiled chin. "Just like an eagle when you were flying. You honestly did. And the landing…"

"Yes?"

"You looked just like an eagle when you were landing."

Looking away, blushing, the un-feathered places of his face had turned beet red. "Really?"

I held him close to my face, the importance of all this needing to be stressed. "I mean, it couldn't get any better than this. Okay?"

He'd broken eye contact with me again, looking away. "But I made a fool of myself when…"

I wouldn't let one little problem wreck this historic day for us. "You did a wonderful job. It was your first time out."

He'd shifted from one leg to the other, listening intently.

I went on, trying to be helpful. "I think next time you should make a flight plan. And…"

Here, Kiki had stood up to shake out his wings in anticipation of next time.

"You know, go that route. But you did look like an eagle."

"Can we go see real eagles today? You know, at that place they all hang out at."

Dubuque. His suggestion had blown me away. I didn't think he'd been listening when Jeff and I had discussed that earlier in the day. No wonder birds can fly south for the winter. And we can't fly at all.

I'd shaken my head. "I don't think we should do that. I…"

He'd blinked his little gray beady eyes. "Why not?"

"No. You…"

"Please?"

"Okay. Eh, ah…" I stammer on, exasperated and looking for a way to explain it all.

"Eagles need a river!"

And I'd need to explain to Jeff what's going on here. "There's a place by the Mississippi River. It's not far from here."

Kiki's feet had gone hot with anticipation. "We could drive there. Pack a lunch."

No way was this bird ready to lunch with the eagles. A fledgling his size, he'd end up *being* lunch. I'd have to take a stand without letting him know why. Without hurting his young ego. Without having to explain the birds and the bees of predator and prey to him this soon.

"I don't want to. I'd rather stay home today."

"It's right over there." Kiki had leaned forward, adamantly pointing west with his beak. "Fine. Don't come with. With my inner radar, I'll find it alone."

"It's that…"

"Way," he finishes for me.

"I know. I know. It's due west. And um, what he wants to do is go to this lock on the Mississippi River."

"I could fly with the eagles there."

"Where the eagles fly. And they get their food there. And um, he wants to fly with the eagles there. But you know what? I don't think you're ready yet. I…"

"Why not?"

Because you'd be lunch. I won't say it though. "It's just me. Maybe it's just me. But I really don't, I don't think you are. Your feet are hot right now because you were scared."

"Never!"

I back off. "All right. You weren't scared." Rolling my eyes, I listen to him.

"I flew and everything."

"I know. You weren't scared. I was, I was more scared for you." I look up at the sky looking for all manner of predators. For crows. And hawks. And yes, for eagles. Who do fly by occasionally. "I mean, this is scary to be out here in our high tech flight cage."

"Flight cage?"

Caught repeating the same lie, I eat humble pie again. And I must giggle, smiling down at this miniature life form sitting on my finger. "I mean our Coleman picnic tent. Okay? So we'll go in and maybe eat some cold food 'cause you're warm right now. And uh, and then, we could come out and, and try this again later maybe.

When…" I rub at the dried crust still soiling face. "Long after you ate."

"Can we just forget that?"

I start to laugh. "I think, perhaps. Okay?"

Kiki, having nuzzled the tip of my thumb with his beak, doesn't have to say he loved me. I knew he did.

Dipping my head towards the bird, my heart swelling, I say it out loud. "I love you too." Repeating this, I've become a babbling fool. A fool very much in love with this tiny mess of feathers. And down. And pink skin. All teetering on my fingertip just then. "Kiki!" I just love saying his name to him. "Kiki? Kiki?"

His head popped up, having seen something that took his full attention away from me. "A mosquito!"

I look up, trying to hone in on what he's seeing. Then we're dizzily following the miniscule flying thing together. "Oh. Whoa. You're right. There's mosquitos in here. Ha!" I look around at the screened walls around us. "This thing doesn't even work. It doesn't even work." And because it doesn't, it becomes a teachable moment. "We could always eat 'em." I say it again, laughing, pulling his puny leg—but not really. "Okay, Kik. Let's go in. Let's go in. Because I love you."

Kiki had touched the tip of his beak to my nose before sitting down in my hand. Exchanging secrets to each other in this very private moment, his beak against my lips, I coo and babble and become an idiot again.

"Are you my baby?" More of this ensuing, I listen to him intently. "Maybe some other time we could try that. All right?"

Kiki won't give it up. "I could make it to the river."

I tell Jeff again what's going on. "He wants to fly outside the cage. But I don't think we're ready. 'Cause we're not eating, we're not eating on our own yet." And if Kiki got lost, released too soon, he'd starve to death.

Kiki leans into me, all his attention on my upper lip. "You've got a little something—right there."

"I know. You did that. It was nice, wasn't it? Good aim. Good aim." Giggling, I'm only doing it to show it's not really a problem, whatever's still hanging on my upper lip. "Good aim. All right. So, we'll go in and, we could watch TV." Kiki called my Fire device a TV because I really didn't own a television. "Or listen to music."

"The river." He wouldn't let this idea go now.

"I have an idea though. We could go watch the hummingbirds in the window again. That was fun."

"But I won't be outside with them."

"It's not as good as being outside flying with them—'cause they're like helicopters." I look to Jeff. "That's what he thought anyway."

"He?"

Calling me out on this gender thing again, I do believe Kiki's only playing with me. "She. Sorry." And, placing him back on a branch, I'd retrieved his feeding syringe. "See, you're still eating like a baby even though you're outside. Yeah."

"Why can't I eat on my own yet?"

I'd rubbed the tip of my nose against his chest. "'Cause that's how it goes sometimes. So you're not ready. I know you want to be an eagle."

"I hear a *but* coming."

"But eagles don't eat out of 10cc syringes with the tip cut off. It's just a fact of life."

He gets antsy. "How long will it take, growing up?"

"Once you get over this, once you get weaned, you know. Then we can think about releasing you. Okay?"

He'd cocked his head towards the screen wall. "But listen to all that out there. Just listen!"

I do, the chatter of other birds beaconing his attention away from me. "I can hear the birds. I know. They're out there. But that doesn't mean you have to be out there. You're just not ready yet. Okay?"

Having turned his back on me in silence, it just proved he wasn't ready to hear the truth.

"All right. You can ignore me all you want. But you're not. You're not ready."

He still wouldn't turn to face me, hurt. Angry.

"You can turn a cold wing on me, it doesn't mean you're ready I'm sorry to say. But you will be soon. You will be soon. You'll be out here. You'll be having fun with the rest of the birds. You'll find grackles..."

Suddenly, the little head snaps my way.

"I mean—eagles. All right. Eagles to play with. And we'll have a ball. We'll have a ball."

Thinking all this over, Kiki had softened to me again. The syringe shook in his face, he can't eat another bite. And it appears that all this waiting to grow up has grated on his nerves.

But if he doesn't eat, he'll never have a chance. The syringe's tip being shook before his beak, he still doesn't feel like eating. "Come on. Open, open." I try to make the squeaky sound he always makes when he begs to eat. "Ahhhh. Ahhhh. Ahhhh."

"I'm just not hungry. After the doodle catastrophe."

Trying to remain upbeat despite this small failure, I'll talk only of how we had fun out here. "Okay. That was fun." And once again, he's sitting on my finger. "Okay. So we'll go in."

"We'll go in."

"All right. Let's do it." Turning in the direction of the house, I lift my hand so Kiki can jump to my shoulder. Little wings fluttering against my ear, he makes himself at home there. And I know we won't need the carrier again. "We're going to go in."

"I love shoulder rides."

"Okay."

Walking ever so carefully so he won't fall off towards the tent's zippered opening, to the great big world outside it, I have to laugh. For, despite all his best efforts at being a magnificent, fearless eagle—Kiki's little feet have hung on for dear life.

Still just my little bundle of feathers after all is said and done.

CHAPTER 11 (VIDEO 11)
BIRDSONG

June 10, early evening

Kiki was getting stronger each and every day, flying from perch to perch in the big cage in my room. Still refusing to eat on his own yet, I'd put out dishes of hydrated dry cat food and meal worms all over the place. I could hope. A big water dish set there, he at least could drink on his own now. He'd taken a sip quite by accident once while throwing the water around, playing.

And while he still sang a cappella in front of his mirror when the vacuum cleaner was on, sometimes he sang without it too. Which meant that both of us now knew what his song sounded like. So it was time to match his voice up with the type of bird he may be. I'd be treading on thin ice today. I knew that.

But Kiki had this *chuck-chuck* sound he did on occasion that sure sounded like a grackle's chuck-chuck. So—I had a plan to play bird songs on my computer for him. To pigeon hole him. To find out once and for all what type of bird exactly we had here.

By playing bird songs for him, I could prove to *him* what kind of bird he was. I guess I just wanted him to face reality. About the whole eagle thing. I'd hoped to urge him to accept his lot in life. And at this young age too so as to not be hurt worse down the road. Not all of us could be eagles, after all.

But Kiki had other ideas, of course.

He'd made himself at home on my desk. His toes curled around his roost made of birch, the window at his back was full of trees. Birds. And yet, his tiny gray eyes stayed glued to my laptop's screen.

Waiting to begin our quest to see which bird's song his matched, his widely spaced eyes wore a fiercely determined look. He wanted to get to the bottom of things too. But only to prove to me that he was actually an eaglet.

So, the both of us stuck in the house, daylight waning through the window at our backs, Kiki had hunkered down. Out to uncover the truth at all costs, he was out to prove to me that he was indeed an eagle. And so the task before us proved to be doubly earth shattering.

A young bird's heart about to be broken, I began.

My thoughts whirring in my brain, palms sweaty, I'd surfed to a university's bird site. Navigating to the Common Grackle page, Kiki's eyes scanned it. Widening in fear, they'd settled on the song clip tabs.

"Kiki has asked me to go to the Cornel Lab of Ornithology." Nervously fidgeting on his perch, I stroked his back to calm him. "Right Kik?"

"Right." But he'd turned his back to the computer, fraught with worry.

"And we're at the *All About Birds*. So he can hear bird sounds. So he can prove to me who he is. And I'd brought up Grackle first." And here I'd rolled my eyes to make light of all this for Kiki's sake.

It didn't work. "But I'm not a grackle." The fledgy then flapped his wings, nervously slapping them at his sides repeatedly.

I'd plowed on, hoping to get this over and done with. "And we're going to listen to the Common Grackle."

"Common? Common?"

"And we're. And...and.." I'd stammered on, trying to think. I was about to break a young bird's heart.

"Common?" he'd spluttered again.

Knowing that he might have guessed I surely was insinuating that he was something *common*, my own heart shattered right along with his. How would I fix this? How would I let him down easy after hearing the truth? There was no way. And so this whole event would just be awful from here on in for us both.

"There's nothing common though..."

He leaned towards me, wings still flapping nervously. "Common?"

"I, I didn't, I didn't mean common."

The little bird just shook his head forlornly. He'd looked sideways at me, distrustfully. "Yes you did."

I shook my own head. "I, I didn't."

He cut me off cold. "Didn't you say common?"

"Did you...?" I'd stopped. Exasperated, I didn't know where I was going with this.

He'd been irrevocably hurt. "Eagles aren't common."

Backpedalling from the truth was never my forte. "Nah, I didn't mean anything..."

"Too late, Mom."

"No. Common, it's, it's just the name of it. It doesn't mean..." I cleared my throat, took in a deep breath and fluttered my eyelashes. Trying to find the right words to smooth over this little misunderstanding, I knew it couldn't be done. "It doesn't mean it's actually..."

"Common?"

I'd given up. I'd play the song clips on the internet site. And I'd let those songs speak for themselves. "Okay, here we go. Here we go."

Kiki's head turned momentarily towards the screen. Waiting for the anvil of reality to fall, I pushed the button to make the grackle's song play. As it played, our eyes locked, confusion coursing through us both.

When the grackle's song came to the whistling part at the end, Kiki seemed shocked. Tossing up his wings, he'd skittered to the furthest edge of his perch. Either scared witless by the sound. Or stunned by the heavy realization he'd sounded exactly like it.

I let him know that the shockingly shrill blast was incredibly beautiful nonetheless. "Ah! Oooh. Pretty. That was the Common Grackle. And now, we're going to go to, the eagle because…"

Looking down momentarily at his toes, Kiki's head suddenly snapped back up to view the eagle page. His eyes stayed on the photo of the eagle, bigger than he was. "It'll sound like me, the eagle."

I'd touched his beak with my finger to garner his utmost attention, directing my words at Jeff. "Because, um. You know, he, he thinks he's an eagle."

Kiki looked quizzically at me, head tilted sideways. "Because, maybe, I am an eagle. Because if I'm not, life isn't worth living."

He wasn't going to make this easy on me, was he? "*IS* an eagle. *IS* an eagle. Okay? And we're going to go to the eagle sounds." Moving my curser to the eagle song clip button, I'd hovered there. "And now I'm going to hear the sounds."

Pressing the button this time around, Kiki's eye and my eyes both searched one another's. And as the eagle sang its incredibly grating excuse for a song, I'd been relieved Kiki's voice sounded nothing like this. But a cold chill ran up my spine nonetheless. It was over. With a heavy heart, I'd proved it once and for all to Kiki. That he was no eaglet. And I'd smiled to soften the blow.

But with a straight face, with total conviction, Kiki stared at me right back. "Didn't I tell you? That's me all right. I'm an eagle. I sound exactly like that."

But he hadn't. He hadn't. The smile fell from my face straightaway. "There's just one problem. You..."

"I sound just like that eagle. I do."

But Kiki didn't. He didn't sound like an eagle at all. And it was time for the truth. Feeling like a deflated balloon, the air in my lungs failing me, a small prayer coursed through me. *Dear sweet Jesus, with this bird's innocent eyes upon mine, give me strength.*

I was about to hit Kiki hard with the unvarnished truth. "You don't sound anything like that." I followed his eyes, darting from me to the screen and back again. "You sounded like the first one."

"I sounded like the second one. And if I didn't, I could."

We were in trouble here, Kiki in denial like this.

"Well, I. No, I'm..." I reached out to him with a single shaking fingertip on order to find common ground again. To make a truce, if possible. "I know you could sound..."

He'd only moved away from me. "You never believed in me, Mom."

"No." I'd pulled my hand back, not knowing how to patch things up here. "I didn't mean to be—snotty." I reached out for him and took him upon my finger. I'd held him lovingly up to my face, like always. "I know you can sound that way if you want to."

"But?" He'd crouched down, steeling himself against me. Against the hand stroking his back. That hand begging for mercy.

I stumbled on. "I know, I know that you could do the eagle sound. But I, I don't know if it'll work."

The truth coming, he looked around for a place to fly off to. "No. Let me go."

I wouldn't let him go. My fingers wrapping gently around him, I held him right up to my eyes. "If sounding like an eagle will make you one." I'd wish that for him. But, having hurt him, his eyes misting up, I gulped back the pain. "Do you know, do you know what I mean?"

"What's wrong with being an eagle?"

"I didn't—I don't want to bring—I'm just trying to be realistic."

"Why?"

Still stroking his back, I'd hoped he'd forgive me for playing the songs to him. And see the light. And let me off the hook here.

I'd try harder. "So we don't. We don't get hurt, when, you know, over anything? And I thought that maybe this, this would show you…"

He stood on my finger and angrily shoved his face my way. "What? Show me what?"

"That…" I'd run plum out of words. "Well. I'm. I know…"

"I'll sing the dumb eagle song. Right here. Right now."

"You can. All right." But if he had, it would only be in imitation of an eagle. "I'm sorry to hurt you like this." I'd held back the tears for his sake, watching him pace nervously on my finger. "I am. But I, I wanted you to, to just, keep your options open. Like you said at the beginning."

"I never said that."

"You were going to keep your options open. Right?"

"I did. And I'm still an eaglet." He'd kept looking away from me, unable to face me. Or the truth.

Kiki, not listening to reason, I kept hammering away at the options thing. "And this, this was keeping them open. I think."

Kiki looking down again, crushed, remaining silent, this hadn't been worth it. Hearing the truth had broken his spirit. And it had been all my doing, hurting him like this.

Smiling again, trying to soften the blow, I had to make this work. "So that's where we stand now. He kind of sounds like a grackle," I'd said to no one in particular this time around.

Kiki's steely eyes boring into mine, it was over all right. "Why was I ever hatched in the first place?"

I'd wondered—how could I ever make him see? That, when the time came to release him into the wild, he could not try to flock with eagles. For if he tried, it would mean certain death. My little baby would become a mere meal to a predator that was a thousand times bigger than him. And I couldn't let that happen, feeling hurt or not. I was in hell. Just hell. Reason for Kiki wouldn't enter into it. Not yet anyway.

And yet, I gave in to his hopes. His dreams.

I'd exclaimed to the world—"Eagle!" My adrenaline having spiked out of control, thinking Kiki's statement about never being hatched would kill me, I'd backed off at all costs. "He sounds just like an eagle."

Kiki had gotten all excited. "Did I? Did I?"

I nod furiously his way. Sometimes in life, the truth just shouldn't matter. "You did. You sounded just like an eagle." And I was out to prove it to him. "Here. Listen. Listen again."

This time when I'd played back the eagle's screechy song to Kiki, I nodded at him. "Yeah."

Now it was his turn to backpedal. "Are you sure I sing like that?"

Listening intently, I nod again. "Yep! That's Kiki!"

Kiki laughing with joy, it was so infectious, I'd joined in right along with him. With him being happy, I was happy again. And that's all that should ever matter.

"That's Kiki! That's my Kik!"

He stood taller on my finger. "Do I sing like that really?"

"Yeah. Okay!" I'd touched my nose to his face, tickled by the wild baby down still spiking out from his temples. "Baby." Hugging him lightly inside the hollow of my chin, I'd broken into boop chatter nonsense baby talk. "He's my baby. He's my eagle eaglet. He's my eaglet."

Tears flooded the bird's eyes. "I'm an eagle! I'm an eagle!"

"Yes you are. Yes you are. You're my eaglet." I'd hugged him to my face as he stood there, blinded by emotion. "Yes you are. Yes you are." I'd then placed him back onto his little perch. The both of us—exhausted from this emotional roller coaster. "There you go. Whoop!"

Falling off, he'd jumped back upon my finger. "Do eaglets lose their balance?"

Lifting him to my face as I got out of my chair, I could see that getting Kiki into adulthood would not be easy. Right about then, I'd have just settled on seeing him eat a meal worm all on his own. Nobody ever promised anybody that growing up would be the easiest thing to do.

But for an abandoned baby bird who didn't know his real mother, it would be extra hard. On the both of us.

CHAPTER 12 (VIDEO 12)
STAR SPANGLED BIRDY

June 12, late afternoon

I'd had Kiki for about two weeks now. Which meant that he was somewhere about three weeks old. Give or take a few days. Finally, for the last five days, I'd finally gotten a full night's sleep. It was a conscious decision to so.

Because at day nine, it had dawned on me that if I didn't get a whole night of sleep, I'd just up and die. There were signs I'd most likely shared with Seal Team Six.

My heart had pounded mercilessly in my chest. And I was so forgetful, I'd stood in the shower with a bar of soap in my hand—unable to figure out what to do with it. But though I'd stopped the nighttime feedings, I somehow got the bird here.

Kiki was finally a gawky tween.

A mixture of down and dull, half grown in feathers, he was still nowhere near eating on his own yet. But the time was getting closer. Today he'd at least picked up a piece of dry cat food that had been soaked in water. Though if truth be told, instead of eating it, it instead became an excellent Frisbee.

The small disc of cat food smacking the wall, he'd laughed when it stuck there. Like a twelve year old who'd just toilet papered somebody's trees, he'd thrown another. When Kiki was done sticking all his food on the wall, he got bored. He really wanted to go outside.

Or, more specifically, he'd wanted to have a picnic supper in the screened in tent.

On the way out, spying my father's old flag folded on a table, he'd wanted me to bring it with us. After hanging it up on the tent's wall before the branch he'd perched on, he was then ready to eat.

The flag request didn't seem that unusual. Not coming from somebody who was sure he was hatched to be an eaglet. Eagles and all things patriotic did go hand in hand after all. Or rather—wing in wing.

The tent at our backs, our emotions had run high.

As Kiki downed yet another syringe of food, he'd squawked madly for more. At this age he'd become a bottomless pit. "Faster. Feed me more. Faster!" Hunkering down, wings doing that flapping thing baby bird's do when they're fed, he couldn't stand to wait another second.

"Hang on. I'm on it." I had to laugh, unable to refill the syringe fast enough.

"Hurry up."

"I'm on it, Kik." Feeding him, so healthy, I secretly gave my thanks to Jesus for giving me him. For this miraculous day. For the flag at our backs.

Jeff stepped inside the zippered opening, horning in with his lens again. Seeing the flag there, he'd asked me what was going on—the Fourth of July being weeks away.

"We're with Kiki. Outside. In our high tech flight ca..." Those innocent eyes suddenly on me, I couldn't lie in front of him. "I mean our—he hates it when I lie—I mean, our Coleman picnic tent. And..."

Kiki, swallowing his food, had interrupted me. "Can you sing that flag song for me?"

The Star Spangled Banner. I'd sung it once to him when he'd still been in his plastic nest.

"What? Nah." I was sure I'd goof up the words. Being put on the spot like this, I didn't want to attempt making a fool of myself. Well, a bigger fool than usual anyway. "You want me to sing? You want me to sing?" If I stammered long enough, he just might give this up.

His beak moving as he swallowed, his words seemed garbled. "Sing please?"

Exasperated, I'd try to get out of it again. "You're supposed to be singing. You're the bird." I'd mimicked his sound best I could. "Aren't you supposed to be singing. Squawk? Squawk?"

Shutting up till I started, he wouldn't even open his beak for more food.

"Oh. Well." Giggling I knew how stubborn he could be. "I've a, crossed a line here." I waved the syringe in his face but Kiki wouldn't say a thing. I'd try again. "Aren't you supposed to be singing? You're a bird. You're supposed to be singing, not me."

Not a word.

I put down the syringe, giving up. "Okay. He wants me to sing. What do you want me to sing." Surely, I could sing maybe Darth Vader's theme song again—no words involved.

"The flag song."

He wouldn't let this thing go. "Oh. Sure. He's a patriotic eaglet. Because of…"

The bird had interrupted with, "How I am a patriotic eagle."

"Aren't you? Aren't you? Yes, yes, yes." Having noogied him with my forehead, I so loved this funny little guy. "He's patriotic. And he wants to fly around a stadium. Like an eagle." I wink, proud as any mother of her little ones ambitions.

All Kiki heard were the words *like an eagle*. "I really will be an eagle. And I really will fly around a stadium. And I'll inspire people."

And so there it was. My common little grackle truly had pinned all his hopes on becoming an inspiration. An eagle. A star spangled birdy.

Yet, I was still stuck on babbling baby talk to him. "'Cause he's going to grow up and be an eagle. And um, aren't you? Aren't you going to grow up and be an eagle?"

Kiki having stepped up onto my finger, I was overjoyed when he'd kissed my hand anyway. He was becoming quite the teensy feathered gentleman. He was like a little knight—but not very much closer to being an eagle. Weighing no more than an ounce or two, I'd remain inwardly skeptical.

And I still didn't want to sing. "So he wants me to sing—that song?"

It had become his favorite. "Why not that song?"

Because maybe it had an impossibly wide range? "That song? That song?" I nod to the stars and stripes gently waving at our sides. "You want me to sing that song? That one?"

"Please." Making himself comfortable on my hand, waiting for me to begin, he gives me his full attention.

Being so insistent, I cannot refuse him. So, gearing up to sing, I wait, a car fast approaching. "Should we wait for the car to go by?" Kissing my thumb, I rub his back. "Aren't you my baby?" Talking absolute gibberish to him for a few seconds, I so hope he's forgotten the request.

No such luck. "I'm waiting."

"You want me to sing then to you? That song? That song?" I go for the low note at the beginning and start to gag. To cough. To hack out of control.

"What happened?"

"I'm allergic to you."

I see the sides of his beak go up in a smile. "You won't get out of this that easy."

"That song? Do you know what kind of range that song has? It's got like a four octave range. I'd like to hear you sing it."

"Would you please get serious here."

"Okay. Here we go." I try again, clearing my throat, wetting down my cotton mouth. And I'm trying to get serious though I don't feel like being serious at all. "Oh say can you see…"

Kiki had gone all shy on me like he always did when actually being sung to. His eyes moving off towards the flag, he'd gotten all choked up.

I go on. "By the dawn's early light. What's so proudly we hailed, at the twilight's last gleaming."

Kiki kissed my lips ever so lightly with the tip of his beak. His face in close, I can feel his warm breath on my face.

"Whose broad stripes and bright stars, through the perilous night, o'er the ramparts we watched…" Kissed again. "Were so gallantly streaming."

Pecking my hand gently in teensy little kisses of thanks, he was so happy.

"And the rocket's red glare."

Kiki moving back to my lips, he'd kissed me very hard.

"The bombs bursting in air." And I had to laugh. "Gave proof through the night, that our flag was still there."

Squawking madly, Kiki actually said, "Yippee!" And then kissed every one of my fingertips in pure joy.

"Oh say doth that star spangled banner yet wave."

He'd attached his beak to my fingertip, tickling me.

"O'er the land of the free. And the home of the…"

Touching the tip of his beak to my mouth, he so loved the coming word—singing it with me. "Brave."

And so I'd joined in, singing it with him. "Brave!"

"Was that all for me, Mom?"

"That was for you." But now it was Kiki's turn, not about to get off that easy. "Now you have to fly around the stadium like a patriotic eagle." I'd repeated myself, moving my hand, with him on it, towards the flag. "Come on. We're going to fly around the stadium like a patriotic eagle. You ready?"

"But the wind's just come up. Hard!" Not even eagles would fly in hard wind.

But this wind wasn't that hard at all. "One. Two. Three."

Flying the two feet back to his stick, I applaud madly. Giving him a much needed chance to get back his breath, I'd then moved far away from him. I'd wanted him to think about all this. The flag. The Star Spangled Banner. The impossible burden it would be to have to look after this flag. This country.

But being a patriotic eagle, that's exactly what he'd planned on doing.

Kiki took this moment to silently reflect on all he'd aspired to become. For America was not only my land. It was his land too— this little tiny creature. And while he'd accidentally lightened his load again before the flag, haven't we all done as much? Haven't we all, before the red, white, and blue at one time or another, accidentally dishonored it?

Kiki stood there before the gently waving flag and thought about the burden he'd taken on. By aspiring to be an eagle.

Tiring work, he'd turned towards me. "Being patriotic made me hungry."

I feed him again, an eaglet needing his strength. "There's my baby." After a few dumb seconds of me cooing utter nonsense, I'd backed off. "Are you done? Kik! Kik!"

He was done. It was now time to grow up. Grow up though down still stuck out all over his head. It was time to stand proudly before his flag. All alone. On nothing more than his own two teensy little chicken feet.

So there, before the flag of his forebirds, he stood dreaming.

He'd dreamt that one day he'd inspire someone else to love the flag as much as he did. To love the country as much as well. Watching this display, I heard America The Beautiful play lushly in my head. I'd even imagined tiny fireworks bursting all around Kiki too. Craning his head at each fiery burst of color, Kiki seemed to see them as well.

The both of us, having somehow experienced the awe and wonder of our America. Together.

CHAPTER 13 (VIDEO 13)
OUR BIG EAGLE DISCUSSION

June 22, noon

I sat outside in the new red, white and blue American flag camp-
chair. The one that Kiki saw online and made me buy for him. The
day was warm and comfortable. Though overcast, I could see the
glowing iridescence of a male grackle developing in his feathers.

A *beautiful* male grackle.

Kiki, perched on the chair's back ledge, had grown fidgety.
Getting up. Sitting down. Getting up again. With him unable to
relax, it was as if he knew what was about to take place. Having half
expected this—Our Big Eagle Discussion—he'd wanted no part of
it.

I needed his utmost attention for this conversation to have any
impact at all. "Kiki?"

He snapped at me. "No." Then he pinched the fabric of the chair
between his beak, trying to hold it all back, the tirade. "I said I don't
want to talk about it." His eyes coursing over the white stars
smattering the dark blue ground at his feet, he suddenly looked up at
me. "I'm an eagle." He looked back down at the flag, the emotions
welling within him. "An eagle."

I didn't know how to proceed. I didn't know how not to hurt
him. The tiny bird was seated on the back of my chair, mere inches
from my face. Hearing the truth from me would be like taking a
bullet at close range.

But Kiki was now eating on his own. He'd thrown back his first meal worm about a week ago. Vocalizing before his mirror like an opera star, even his voice had gotten more mature.

A full blown teenager now, he was also embroiled in a teenager's angst. Angst he'd had a right to experience just like anybody else. All the confusion being a learning process, he'd earned it. And I'd gotten him here—proud he'd made it.

I'd tried to open the talk gently, peering over my shoulder at him. "I know the flag means a lot to you. And that you think you're an eagle."

"Mom. Don't even go there."

I plowed on. "But I think it's time we had the eagle talk."

"I don't need to hear this."

But he did need to face this sooner of later—the fact that he was hatched a common grackle. "Kik? Kiki?"

Nearing me, he sat down right next to my cheek. "Please? Just, stop."

"No." I wouldn't let him stop me this time. I wouldn't fall for those big eyes upon me. Not like the last time I'd tried to confront him with the truth about his being a grackle.

"Some other time then?" He'd whispered the words into my ear. Then he'd waited there, dreading this, while I turned to face him.

"All right. You might think it's easy to, just, you know. Keep pushing it aside—the facts." I'd faced him down. Faced all the dread in his eyes, steeling myself against it. "But the facts are that you just..." How could I say this tactfully? "You don't have a white head. Or a white tail."

"I will though." No, he was not about to give up his dream willingly.

I'd waded in yet further. "And so, I think you might..."

127

"Don't say it." He stood up, upset, for the merest of seconds. Then he pecked nervously at the chair's fabric again.

I'd gulped once, nearly unable to go on. " I know you don't want me to say it. I know you don't." That he may not be an eaglet after all was said and done.

"What about the stars?" He looked over my face with great intensity.

And I'd looked away. "I know the stars mean a lot to you." On the flag. "But…" I let out an exasperated sigh. Pulling myself together. For Kiki's sake. "The truth of the matter is…"

Kiki stood up and took a step closer to me. This much closer to hearing the truth, his eyes had misted over.

I licked my lips, killing time. Waiting to find a better way to say this, there was no better way. So I'd just blurted it out to get it all over and done with. "You might not be an eaglet."

Kiki said nothing in his own defense. His chest feathers puffing out in an attempt to look larger than he actually was, my heart nearly failed me.

I'd plowed on. "You're four weeks old." He could even be a few days older. His birthday—or hatchday—could be off by a few days. I had no way of knowing when he'd actually cracked his way out. "And…"

He'd pretended he wasn't paying attention to me. If he didn't hear any of this, it would somehow go away. The truth of the matter.

"I've had you for three." Weeks.

"I helped you lose weight."

Truer words were never spoken. "And I know I'd lost ten pounds." All the hard work keeping up with Kiki, he'd actually been good for me. "Well…"

Proudly prodding me with an open beak, he'd helped me accomplish the impossible. I'd been trying to lose weight for the longest time to no avail.

But I wouldn't let that bit of good fortune deter me. "I know. You, you gave that to me. It was a real nice present." One that made me so happy, I'd somehow filled the tiniest of these hard won seconds with a small laugh. "But um…"

Kiki had moved his body closer to my eyes. Dreading the coming words in silence, he'd hunkered down. And waited. In silence.

"The fact of the matter is, Kiki, that—you might not be an eagle."

He looked me right in the eye, pressing towards me even further. "But I am an eagle. You'll see."

"Kik, come on now." Feeling guilty for breaking his heart, I'd broken eye contact with him. Looking down at my lap, I focused on my uneasy hands, folded there. Gently shaking with remorse, I hated myself for pressing this on him.

"But I'd tried so hard." He stared forward with resolute conviction.

"I know. We gave it our best shot. But sometimes, you know, life just gets in the way."

Kiki turned away again, wings dropping at his sides. "Then I just give up. On everything."

It seemed there's been no way to make this bird see that, despite his having given up on one dream, another dream may present itself. A dream even better than the old one. But Kiki was young, so young. It was painful to watch, reality striking him down at this tender age—with his whole life ahead of him.

I tried to be upbeat for his sake. "We still are going to have a wonderful summer."

"What about the parades?" His heart set on walking in parades, he'd so wanted to inspire patriotism in people. His dream falling to pieces all around him, he'd paced on the back of the chair nervously. "Only an eagle can draw a crowd."

"Parades I don't know about. I..."

"I'll never fly again."

Putting the screws to me, this bird, I'd backed down again to spare his feelings. "Well, okay. If you want to do parades..."

"Do eagles catch bugs at parades?"

"...And catch bugs during parades—just to show that you're an eagle." I'd smiled to make it all seem possible, his walking in parades. Then I hit him with a bit of truth again. Out to soften the blow while making him see the light. "I think that eagles like water. And um...

He got up and moved towards me. "But, I don't like water. Yet."

"I know." Hello? We'd touched foreheads ever so lightly. "I think eagles like water. And..." Finally listening to me, I went for it. "They catch fish. And you catch insects."

"I could catch fish."

"You're kind of small to be catching like a, a thousand pound salmon."

He stared blankly. "A thousand pound what?"

"I, it's true." Though in all likelihood, grackles were adept at catching itsy bitsy crawdads. Still, the truth about Kiki being a grackle needn't be rubbed in at this point too harshly. As it was, I could barely speak at this point, having broken his spirit so callously. "I know you don't want to hear it."

"Stop then." Kiki, about to jump from the back of the chair, he'd had enough.

And if I didn't fix this somehow now, I might lose his heart forever. "Kiki." I had to patch things up between us. "Kiki, I love you—as a grackle." He had to realize that I'd love him no matter what he was.

"Wait just one minute here." He'd stood up to show me how tall he could be. "Look. Look at how big I'm getting."

"Kik—your head's turning blue. It does…it's not…"

"That's it. I'm leaving home."

"Okay. I'm sorry I said it. I'm ssss…" Hissing out a bunch of nothing, I had no idea what I'd wanted to say. No idea how to fix this mess I'd made. "I didn't mean anything by…" It.

Kiki surmising that I had indeed, he'd turned all the way around. He was trying to make it obvious that he was ignoring me.

"You don't have to turn your back on me." But his having done so, and on purpose, that hurt. Terribly. His tail feathers brushing against my face, I'd gotten all choked up. Fighting back the tears, not an easy thing to do.

But when he wouldn't turn around again to face me, the sun hit fully on his feathers. And by being his obstinate self, he'd only made it all too obvious. The truth.

"Kik? Your tail's blue too. No, I'm sorry." Giggling nervously to show him that this was all small potatoes, he didn't buy it either.

He'd only turned and faced me again. "Will you love me if I'm not an eagle?"

"I love you anyway. It doesn't matter that you're a grackle. I love grackles. Grackles, you could get a lot accomplished in your life by being a grackle. You have high aspirations."

With Kiki's eyes on the sky outside the screened in picnic tent, he'd merely sighed wistfully.

"I know." Looking out at the wide expanse of nothingness with him, we dreamed together—my cheek against his chest. "Look at it out there. It's a big world. It's huge world. And the sky is so vast." I'd looked at him. "And it's all yours. All of it. But I think that we should, show you that maybe, perhaps that…" And I thought the unthinkable.

Hanging out with eagles will get a pipsqueak like you killed.

A beak lunged at my eye. When I'd laughed, Kiki knowing how to lighten the moment, he sat back down, satisfied. "I made you laugh."

"That…" And though I'd laughed, I'd gotten right back to the harsh reality of the task at hand. We'd show, "You're not an eagle. By…" performing some sort of test.

"By doing what? I don't need to test myself."

"By, I know." I rubbed at my nose, all the backed up tears making it run. "Putting you in water."

"What!?"

"Come on." Having placed my finger at his feet, he climbed innocently aboard. Caught up in the sheer force of habit, it was too late to back out then. "We're going to find out, once and for all, Kiki…"

"Water?" Being held to chest level on my finger, he'd absolutely freaked out. "Like I'm a penguin?!"

"I know." But we had to know. "If you're an eagle or not."

"You're not my mother." Jumping off my finger and back onto the back of the chair, this time, he'd kept his back turned on me.

I'd pushed and pushed and pushed. I'd pushed so hard, I'd severed his trust once more. And hadn't I admitted as much to myself? "I did it again."

He'd turned, faced me and plunked back down. Obviously hot under the feathers, he'd seethed, "I'd trusted you."

"I'm sorry. I'm sorry it's going this way. But…"

I'd rubbed at my swollen nose, disgusted with myself. Disgusted with how hard life had to be sometimes. Disgusted with how badly everything was going between us at this impossible age of his.

But he knew that I'd love him even if he'd turned out to be a lowly grackle. He knew that! "Why can't you be a grackle? Grackles are wonderful. They hang out in giant packs." Which all proved without a doubt that grackles—like all birds—are very big on family values.

"Packs?" He'd looked up at the sky in fear—looking for flying wolves.

"Grackle packs. And they look beautiful in the air. And you'll have a blue head."

"I hate blue."

I'd never understand it, why Kiki hated the color he was. "I like blue. Blue is, is part of the flag. The inside of your beak is, is red and white. You'll be red, white and blue. How could you beat red, white and blue?" Like the very chair we'd sat upon.

He sat thinking, quite resolutely too. "I'll be black and white. An eagle."

"You don't have to be just, black and white like an eagle. That's boring." I'd wiped a tear from my eye, all this impossibly hard on me. "I think it's boring."

He peered off into the yard. "You'll see."

At an impasse, if now hadn't been the time to give up this impossible dream, when would that time be? "Do you want to try to swim? And see how it goes? To see if you like water? 'Cause this is like the sure test."

"It is not."

"Eagles love water. I even saw an eagle swimming upstream once with is wings. He was swim…"

Kiki guffawed. "Yeah, right."

"You're not believing me?" I waited for a response.

None came.

My heart sank. "You're not believing me. They do. They can swim. And they can swim *upstream*. And…"

"Mom. Stop it."

I couldn't help but laugh. "They're really good swimmers. So, it would be a good test."

No response. Kiki still had a fear of big water.

"I mean, if you wanted to try it."

Still nothing.

"I think we should do it."

"You do it."

"I think we should go for it."

"You go for it." Then he'd thought about this for a moment. Trying to hide his knees under the puffs of down still at his chest, they must've been knocking. "How deep is it?"

"It's shallow. That's how deep it is. It's not going to be deep. Maybe—one inch? One inches? One inch? You could do an inch."

Getting the cold wing again, the bird looked off into the tree line beyond. Hurt and mad I'd suggested putting him in water.

"You could turn your, you could turn your back on me again. But…"

He really hadn't turned around again at all. He was just ignoring me. "How big is a salmon?"

"Okay. There's no salmon in one inch of water. You don't have to worry about the salmon getting ya. No salmons are going to get ya. Okay?" I placed my finger before his chest for him to step up on. "You want to try it? Come on. Me and you."

Getting onto my finger, his heart wasn't in this at all.

"I'll be with you every step of the way, Kik. We're going to do…"

Bending over, Kiki kissed the palm of my hand. "For good luck."

Making me laugh again, I so loved his pluck, this bird's. "We're going to do water. Are you ready?"

His wings skittered nervously at his sides. "Can't now." Hearing a loud vehicle approaching, Kiki saw an opportunity to back out. And he'd seized it.

The driver doing about eighty miles an hour, I didn't need to make a visual to know who this was. "That's just a milk truck again." I'd waited for it to pass by the house. "There he goes. Okay."

"I'll drown in milk!" Kiki had jumped off my finger and landed on the back of the chair again.

"We're not going to swim in milk. We're going to swim in water. I didn't mean to scare you. Come on now. We're going to do it. We're. Gonna. Do. It."

Forcing him back onto my finger, the time to get this test over with was at hand. The test that would show him he wasn't an eagle. I got out of the chair with Kiki on my finger. The other hand behind him in case he backed out.

Then I'd pep-talked him. "Now let's do it. Come on. Here we go. We're going to see if we're an eagle."

Too late. With the flapping of little wings, the gray ball of feathers squirmed out of my hand. He'd jumped over my shoulder. And then, making his way to the tree branch teetering in the tent's corner, he was gone.

I giggled uneasily for him. "You don't have to be afraid."

But it soon was obvious why he'd jumped. Relief falling through the air, the last minute doodle had landed on the grass with the gentlest of thuds.

"Oh, that," I'd exclaimed, now knowing why he'd flown away. And once again, it all just went to prove how easy it was to misconstrue his actions. "Okay, lighten the load. Okay, now let's try it." Reaching out for him now that he'd finished, I'd held him lightly in my grasp again. "We're going to go in the water. Come on."

Walking over to an aluminum pie tin sitting on the ground, here was our big, bloodcurdling inch of water. His food dishes nearby, a pile of raisins, his soaked cat food, none of it comforted him. For I could feel his hollow boned body quivering with fear in my hands.

"Come on. We're going to try to be in the big river." He'd have to use his imagination. "This is the Mississippi River."

Kiki had looked at the tin, fear in his eyes regardless that it wasn't any big, bad river. "I can't swim!"

It was too late to take no for an answer. "And we're going to be in it." Placing Kiki's body gently into the pie tin, surely he'd overcome his fear of water. "And now you're an eagle!"

Kiki, jumping out immediately, could not believe I'd done this to him. Proved to him that he was no such thing. "How could you? My own mother?"

It appeared that even though I'd won this round, the win felt as shallow as the water in the tin. "Kik, eagles love water." Reaching out to him, he'd hopped away. "Kiki? Kik? Kik! Eagles—Kik?"

He wouldn't listen to reason. Moving silently off in a huff, walking beneath the camp chair, he was out to hide there. For forever.

"Kik? You can't…"

"Leave me alone." He moved off behind his beloved red, white, and blue camp chair to sulk in private.

"What?"

He'd stopped momentarily, hiding there.

"You can't hide forever behind the flag." I neared slowly. "Come here. Come here. Oh, there." Hands out to lift him, he'd jumped through my fingers. "Oh. All right." I'll just talk to Jeff now instead. "He's mad at me now. He's mad at me."

But Jeff remaining quiet, only proved that he was mad at me too.

Out to smooth things over, it wouldn't be easy. "Kik, I didn't mean anything by it. I…" Bending over, I could see him hiding beneath the chair.

From here, he'd looked out at me. "You made a fool of me."

"Kik?"

"What's wrong with being a patriotic eagle?" Trying to perch on the chair leg, he'd slid down it. The act adding insult to injury, it proved how his talons would never be as strong as an eagle's.

And I felt terrible for him. "Kiki? Come out now, honey. Come on."

"Water?" He came out behind the chair and paused there to glare at me. "You dropped me in water?"

My own father had done as much to me when I was a kid. And I just *swam.* "I'm sorry I put you in the water. But, eagles love water." Crouching down, reaching out for him again, he'd looked up at me.

And he'd opened his beak menacingly. "I'll peck you."

Lifting him, I'd laughed without meaning to. At this age, the most Kiki could do with his beak was to give a weak pinch. "We're going to try it again." Nearing the pan of water, I'd use a mind control mantra, repeating swiftly, "Eagles love water. Eagles love..."

When Kiki burst from my hand to fly over to the chair, I'd laughed at his pluck. He did look like a miniature eagle there. Standing so proudly.

I thought I could help further. "Just tell yourself that."

But, the teensy creature, having turned his head towards me, only blinked incredulously.

Wondering how I could be so heartless again, I'd put a hand his way in an effort to make amends. "Come on, Kiki."

With me approaching the back of the chair, he'd turned around to face me. "Don't you Kiki me."

"Kik?" Leaning towards him, he'd at least allowed me to move my face nearer his. And it became time to face the truth. And we both knew it. My voice came out, barely there. All solace and regret. "Eagles love water, Kik."

He walked over to me, his wings up, his voice cracking with emotion. "I know. I know. But why?" When I leaned over to him, he hid his head beneath my chin so I couldn't see his face. His shame.

Allowing him this moment of truth, I rubbed my chin against his back. "Kik, they do."

"Why? Just why?"

"Kiki? Kik?"

I looked down to make sure he was taking this news well. Busying himself—Kiki's beak was tugging at the cross dangling from my neck. Giving him solace too, fashioned from horseshoe nails no less, we at least shared this. Trusting that the bird now had things in perspective, that he'd taken the bad news with a grain of salt, I'd drive the truth home. And be done with it.

"I love you, Kik." And here came the best of what I could impart to him. "I love you even though you're not an eagle." But had he taken this news well? I'd remained unsure because I didn't know if he'd even valued my love anymore. "Kik?"

Nothing to say, he busied himself, wishing this moment had never arrived.

Checking him again, I think this went as well as could be expected. Us having pecked away at the truth like this. I'd broken his heart but he'd made it through. And, rubbing my chin between his wings with a hopeful, "Kiki?" I'd hoped I was forgiven.

Kiki, having turned around quickly, flapped his wings joyously. "If I'm not an eagle, I'm still alive, right?"

Laughing with sheer bliss along with him, we were both so glad. And relieved too, that our worst moment, our moment of eagle reckoning, was now behind us.

"Okay, you might not be an eagle. But..."

My hand before him, Kiki gladly jumped on without a shred of hesitation. And my heart alighted right along with his. The truth was out. And he was okay with it. Holding him before my face, I couldn't believe his simple, beautiful blue majesty.

"You're a beautiful grackle. And you're going to have a blue head." I'd held him to my cheek. "You're going to be red, white, and blue."

He'd jumped from hand to hand, proud of his simple, common self for once joyous moment. "I could fly around with my beak open all the time. So I'll always be red, white, and blue."

I'd concurred, something like electricity snapping at all my nerve endings. "You can't beat that." I'd said it again to him so he'd know the importance of this. "You can't beat that combination."

"I could be just as patriotic as any dumb old eagle." He'd flown back down to the flag chair, waiting there for me to join him.

"Huh?" I had to giggle, so happy that he was seeing the light. Leaning in towards him, his face looked up at mine with anticipation. So I just said it. "I love you. Just remember that. No matter how it turns out. I love you. I will always love you." Lifting him, we'd danced around. All the while I'd sung out that Dolly Parton song that the beautiful, late Whitney Houston had gone on to make even more famous. "I. Eee. I. Eee. I—will always love you."

Flustered, Kiki flew over to the branch propped up against the screen wall. Turning to look at me from afar, his tiny heart swelled in his chest. "I will always love you too, Mom. But as an *eagle*."

CHAPTER 14 (VIDEO 14)
WORM AND GO SEEK

July 17, early afternoon

I'd loved Kiki for seven weeks now. Which meant that he was about eight weeks old at this point. Perhaps a few days older than that even. Living his life torn between two worlds, he didn't quite know that yet. Being both a human and a bird, my baby bird was nearly all grown up. His feathers had grown in black and shiny. His tail, longer every day.

He loved games and toys and new experiences.

The pinch of his beak getting stronger everyday. I'd given him many teething toys to work on it. And all because he'd need a good pinch to crack open a crawfish one day. Kiki seemed to realize this too. He'd started to float his shelled peanuts in his water dish. The bogus hunt gaining more realism when he'd dunked his head underwater to get them I guess.

It seemed that each time I gave Kiki a new teething toy, he'd play with it for hours. Then, when given another toy he'd abandon his previous one—as if sick of it. Going back to the old toy when he'd gotten tired of the new one, this was just one of the bird's many human attributes. And with me saying as much, I'm not being anthropomorphic. Humans are animals too, after all.

So conversely, Kiki had probably witnessed many bird qualities in me without thinking twice about it.

141

His cage floor always littered with toys, he especially loved clamping his beak down on things. A piece of plastic fish-tank tubing. A rubber office finger. An orange washer from a hose.

He also liked knocking around the thin metal tubes of a wind chime. The one I'd hung with a dog clip from his cage's ceiling. Doing this, he'd made music for Jeff and I for hours on end. That is, when he wasn't twirling around the wings of a hummingbird whirligig.

He could be funny too. One day Kiki had found the plastic top to a pen on the floor. Slipping it over his own beak, he hurriedly flew back into his cage. Standing before his mirror to check himself, he knew this was hysterical. This huge beak looking as clownish as a red rubber nose.

But Kiki especially loved shiny things. Stealing a paper clip here, a piece of jewelry there, it was hard to keep these things from him. He had a favorite steel bolt he'd found that he liked to drop to the cage floor. Fetch. And drop again. Doing this over and over again, it was like watching a kid pitching a ball into a wall.

One day he'd eyed my button box. Placing it open before him, I gave him the choice of any button he'd wanted. His big gray eyes meticulously falling over each and every one, he'd finally reached in with his beak. Choosing a miniature flower pot, a yellow bouquet of flowers bursting from its top, he took this button with him wherever he went after that.

One day I'd brought him his treats on a piece of tin foil. His worms. His pieces of egg. Fruit. Tuna. Being shiny and lightweight, he made off with the foil—all the food falling to the floor. Taking a good fifteen minutes to wrestle it away from him, off flying all over the house with it. Scared he could have eaten it, I had to hide all tin foil after this escapade.

After that, he'd found the spent shell casing of an unlit, burnt out votive candle on a table. This, I let him keep. But only after I'd folded its sharp walls in on itself. This tiny tin Frisbee a huge hit, when I'd thrown it through the air, he'd fly off to go get it. Retrieving it, flying back to me to play again, he'd out-dogged dogs on this.

So, after I'd given Kiki all these toys in effort to make his beak in tip top chewing condition, I couldn't very well reprimand him. That is, when he'd used this clamp of death on me sometimes. On my fingers. Or ears. Or toes. Because, if I'd taught him not to bite, what good would that do him after release?

Afraid to defend himself with his beak would mean certain death to a tiny bird like Kiki.

The thought of our release date coming soon, my heart was always heavy with worries of this sort. I knew what the cruel world might hold in store for a tiny defenseless bird who thought he was a big tough eagle.

And so, if he'd nipped me a little too hard in his zeal with the pointy tweezers of his beak, I had to let it go. He'd need to behave this way to survive. His beak his only tool for defense, he'd worked hard to get his clamp strong. And I'd then come up with the perfect last name for Kiki.

Kiki Tweezerbeak.

A feathered terror, Kiki Tweezerbeak had fully lived up to the name. While his hard won nip would serve him well out in nature someday, it certainly was precarious for me sometimes.

When Jeff found us outside in the screened in tent, the day was hot.

Me and Kiki were already sitting down in our favorite American flag chair. Kiki having perched on my wrist, he'd waited for the

143

games to begin. Late in the morning, glorious sunlight streaming down through canopy's white top—I'd turned to the camera like a proud mother.

About to gush about my big baby, the feathers on Kiki's head thoroughly amazed me. Their sheen had alternated from blue to purple to back again. He didn't know it, but Kiki's mesmerizing holographic coloration had it all over an eagle's plain old white and black. He was no longer a little ugly duckling baby—gray and dull with ugly closed pin feathers.

Kiki was gorgeous.

So I said as much to Jeff. "Kiki turned out to be a beautiful male grackle."

But Kiki would have none of it. "A what!" Hurt again by this accusation, the bird had turned away from me. Steamed that I'd said such a thing, I'd have to patch things up. And quickly.

"I'm sorry. He's, he's an eagle." My dearest bird having moved up my arm, his little feet felt overheated. The day reaching upwards of ninety, this worried me. "He's an eagle—it's hot today." As Kiki moved up my arm towards my shoulder, those feathers now showed bright blue. "He's gorgeous."

"Stop it." Embarrassed for us both, he moved up towards my shoulder. Unable to take any more praise, when I'd nuzzled his body with my cheek, he'd lifted off.

"And there he goes." Laughing when he'd flown back towards me, landing on my head, he overjoyed me. "Kik? I have something for you to eat."

Kiki looked down at my hands, at the small container there. "I love this game!"

I'd explain. "We've been playing a game he's been working on. Um..."

"Let's begin!" Kiki was always up for a game that included worms.

"He's been practicing on Xbox. To get, to get his beak-eye co..." Coordination. I peered at him, perched up there on my bangs. His mini talons precariously near my eyes, this took trust. But we'd never played such games for beak-eye coordination. We'd put together bird jigsaw puzzles online instead. "Right?"

"Right." Kiki agreed anyway, not one to call me out on such a lightweight fib. Besides, he was too busy lifting my bangs excitedly with his beak. He couldn't wait for this particular game to start. "Winner takes all."

I'd hurried on with it for his sake. "Yeah. To get his beak-eye coordination together. Working together. And we, we came up with another game. With some wax worms." Bought at the gas station for fishermen, it killed me to see them die like this. But Kiki would have to come first. Thusly, the game. "Called, um..."

Kiki smacked his beak together in anticipation. "Worm And Go Seek."

I repeat this for Jeff's sake. "Worm And Go Seek. And..." Reaching up to remove Kiki, I'd only done it because I'd figured he was due for a doodle again. "Oh, this could be dangerous for me." I'd laugh, feeling little feet tap dancing on my head. "Worm And Go Seek. And so we're going to play it now. A rousing game of Worm And Go Seek." Reaching up for the bird player, Kiki spun around on my head.

Kiki jumped onto my finger and looked around. "Where are they?"

I'd lowered him down to chest height. Holding the container before him with my other hand, I'd showed him. "Here's the worms."

"You already took off the lid?"

I had. Marooned in my lap, I'd soon toss each worm into the grass. Because those were the rules we'd discussed earlier in the day. Rules I'd now make Jeff privy to. "And what we're going to do, is we're gonna…"

"Squawk, squawk!" Eyes honing in on the poor hapless little creatures, Kiki loved wax worms. "Chewy. Cream filled. Hurry."

Before the game had even started, Kiki had leaned over the cup. Trying to grab a worm before I was even ready, his beak was already in the cup.

"You can't get them that…no! Wha…I…eee…you cheated!"

Kiki gobbling down the worm, his eyes narrowed on mine. "I did not."

I held the worm cup far from his face, cheating a sin he should know about. "Kiki, you cheated. I'm supposed to throw them. You're supposed to…"

His teenager self showed me what he'd thought of the rules. "Take that."

Both of us leaning over to watch something hotly sliding down the side of my thigh, I was aghast. "Oh no. Noooo." I'd laughed, hiding my dismay that I'd been both cheated on and pooped on. "Just another poop fatality."

But Kiki hadn't meant to soil me at all. It just happened in all the excitement. "I didn't mean to…" He'd pulled on the buttons of my shirt, embarrassed and nervous.

I'd lead him to believe it didn't matter. "Just another senseless poop fatality. Thanks."

"Let's just play the game, okay?"

I'd moved on for his sake. "So anyway. The point of the game, the object of the game, is to take the worms. And throw them. And then he gets them in the grass. In that way...right?" I'd let him explain.

"I'd learn to hunt." His eyes on the worms in the cup, it seemed unbearable to wait for the game.

"Yeah. He's learned how to forage for worms in the grass. I, I know."

Tugging hard on my shirt, Kiki couldn't stand it any longer. "Will you just give me the dumb worms?"

With all this insistence, all I can do is stutter. "I'll do, I, okay. All right."

With Kiki jumping onto my shoulder, he's about to bite my head off. "Let's go. Now!"

"We'll start. Okay, here's the worms." I'd held the cup up as Kiki slid down my arm towards it. "Here's the worms. And we're going..."

He obviously didn't trust me, flying back up on my shoulder.

I'd reached up for him, shocked his beak is open. "Come here. We're going to...are you hot?"

Reaching down into the cup, he'd faked me out. And scored himself another worm.

"I...you cheated! You cheated aga..."

"I did not."

Stunned he'd done this twice to me, cheated to get a worm, I'd hit my limit. "You cannot trust a *grackle*. You cannot trust a..."

"Eagle!" This screamed, he'd jumped onto the hand holding the worm cup. Taking advantage of how I was no longer paying attention, me laughing at his antics—he scored yet another worm. "I get another point. I'm winning! I'm winning."

"Wait! This isn't the point of the game. You're cheating!" Trying to close the worm container, I'd been unable to do it with

Kiki on my hand. My fingers shaking, I was running out of worms. And fast. He was too quick for me, Kiki. "Hang on. Hang on." Trying to fight off a bird who was faster than me proved useless. "Okay, I'm just going to put the lid on."

"I give up. I give up." Kiki backed off but was probably out to fake me out again. "What are the rules again?"

I'd trusted him again. "All right. The point of the game…" Kiki having knocked the cup into my lap, I retrieved it and held on tighter. "…is that the grackle…"

"Eagle."

This again. "…gets the worms after I throw them in the grass." I'd shaken the worm container before Kiki's face to get his undivided attention. The rules having been outlined out loud, surely Kiki wouldn't try to cut corners again. "All right?"

"This time I won't cheat. I promise."

I thought this over. No, I'd have to distrust him. Worms being something he'd truly loved to eat. "Maybe because he cheated, I should change the rules. Let's do that. Wha…"

"No!" Tapping his beak on the worm's lid, the bird couldn't stand it any longer.

"I'm just going to take the whole thing."

"What whole thing?" Kiki, peering through the lid seemed disheartened. "There's none left."

"The worms are in there." I showed him so he'd believe me.

He didn't. "I'll just check to make sure myself." Having tried to pry the lid off, unable to—he'd only been left more frustrated by the effort.

"He sees them. Eagles aren't stupid. Eagles aren't stupid. Okay?" With Kiki moving up my arm, I'd shaken the container of worms in his face. "Come here." Leaning over, Kiki flying down to a low twig propped at the tent's side, I'd dropped the whole container to the ground. "We're going to put them in the grass. And, there it is." Having left the lid on—this time it was me who'd cheated.

No worms out in the grass for him to hunt down, there was no way for Kiki to get at the prize.

Knowing this, he'd jumped up onto a higher branch, refusing to play. "Real mothers don't cheat."

I'd add more realism to the task at hand—uh, wing. "You're an eagle! These are salmon in a river. Go get them." I'd lifted the cup and held it up to him.

Trying again to pry off the lid, he couldn't. "I've had it with this game."

And I'd rub in his failure to win now. "Go get 'em, Kik."

He'd only moved higher up the branch. "Play by yourself."

Being a spoiled sport, my face pushed into his, I sighed. "You're not going to do it, are you?" Try to open the plastic worm canister.

"Not with you cheating too. No." The bird jumped onto my wrist.

Laughing together, I give up, stunned as the sun danced on his shining feathers. "You are beautiful though." Stoking his ego, I'd so hoped he'd go on to forgive me for cheating right back. "You're a beautiful eagle."

"Do you think so, really?"

With Kiki looking deeply into my eyes, I'd wax on. I'd make it up to him, that he had no arms to open the worms with. "This is a new breed of eagle." Kiki, so excited by my words, had another untimely accident. Feeling something hot hit my thigh, we both look down, mortified. Me being the target, I'd gloss it over again. "Oh no. Just another senseless poop fatality."

Warm feet moving up my arm, Kiki was once again embarrassed for himself. "What's wrong with me?"

Jumping onto my hand, I'd change the subject to fix this problem. "This is a new breed of eagles. They're pygmy eagles. And they have blue and purple heads."

He'd kissed my finger. "Thank you."

Smiling down at him, I'm once again in love. "And they're real shiny." Then I see what he's up to, using my good will to score himself some more worms. "And they cheat at games." But he'd been a good sport, hungry like he'd been. "All right? Okay. You can have the rest."

"I win!"

Taking off the lid, I'd really been just an old softie. Watching him gobble down as many worms as he could, I'd smiled at his good appetite. Truly, I was only happy when he was happy.

"All right. Go ahead. Because I'm a pushover. Mom is a pushover." Seeing him eat the last worm, I'd figured that the game was over with. "All right."

Kiki looked at me suddenly. "There's no more worms." And because of that, he'd bitten my thumb. *Hard.*

"Ouch." Giggling to hide the pain, I'd watched him peck at the cup, trying to find more worms to eat.

"The game can't be over this fast." He seemed stunned.

"Oh, okay. It's over." I'd turned the container upside down and shook it in his face. No worms. Game over. "The game is over. Let's go play Xbox again. What do you say?"

He said nothing, flying up onto my shoulder again, mad.

And I'd laughed on and on. "It's cheaper than buying wax worms. Constantly. All right?" Reaching up for Kiki, he'd jumped onto my hand. But with his beak squeezing my thumb in a mean vice grip, I was sure he didn't know how hard he'd done it. "Ow! Ow!"

Me yelling, he'd let go just as fast. "Am I in trouble?"

"Oh." I wasn't laughing any more, his strength having stunned me. "Boy, you been working on that grip. I know you have. But ooo."

He'd tapped my finger lightly. "I didn't mean to…"

Afraid he'd do it again, I'd held the cup up to him to bite instead. "You want this?" He didn't so I'd lowered it. "No? All right…" But just when I did, he'd pinched my finger even harder than he had my thumb. "Ow! Ow!" The pain sudden and hot, I could feel my face go red. Blood rushing into it, the pain had been absolutely piercing.

He let go of my finger and shook his feathers out. "What?"

"You know, you're not supposed to bite Mom. Biting Mom— ow! Ow! Ow" He had my finger again.

"But it's so funny, you screaming."

My teenager bird truly had no idea how hard he'd hurt me. I was sure of it. The, screaming *OW* a million times over didn't help. He just wouldn't let go. Me being in pain being absolutely hysterical, he'd flown up onto my other shoulder. Guffawing hysterically into my ear, I had to let him. I had to be the bigger bird here.

Red faced, making Kiki get back onto my hand, I'd explain this away as if it meant nothing. "You know, he was such a sweet baby a few weeks ago. We were playing harp. And enjoying ourselves."

"But this is more fun, biting you." That said, Kiki had flown back onto my shoulder.

But I'd looked away, the tension mounting. Though laughing, I secretly feared his newfound strength, glad he'd suddenly flown off me. "I'm going to lose an eye here today." Flying right back on, I squished my eyes shut in a hurry. "I'm going to lose an eye."

He'd gotten back onto my hand without incident though. "I'd never bite your eye."

"All right." Holding him far from my face, I didn't believe him. But I did know how to get revenge. "I'm going to kiss you!"

And I'd done just that. Sneaking a fast one on his black back, I knew he'd hated this. Getting sneak kissed. So I'd reared back before he could snatch out an eyeball.

He'd turned and looked at me from behind his shoulder as I laughed on maniacally. "Lipstick? On my feathers?" He'd hated stealth kisses and lipstick on his feathers.

"Ah! I got him!" With Kiki taking advantage of how I got lost in laughter, he'd sneaked back onto my shoulder. Out to do some mayhem or other, I'd moved forward. Quickly.

Kiki had flown off. Then he'd made it back to the ledge of the flag chair. Out of breath, he'd waited there to see what I'd do next. Then he egged me on. "Dare you to look at me."

"Okay. Where eagles dare." I'd looked around as if not knowing where he'd gone to. "Where are you, honey?" Finding him on the chair behind me to my right, I'd moved my face back a little bit. "Okay, Kik. You wouldn't hit me in the eye, would ya?"

"Never." But he just might, having jockeyed forward into a position where he could.

"You wouldn't hit me in the eye would you? No!" Feeling threatened, getting heat exhaustion, being pooped on. Well, it was all adding up. "I have to go in and clean the…"

"But why?" Kiki had whispered into my ear, worried he'd have to go in too.

I'd reached up for him, the bird getting back onto my hand without incident. "Clean…you know. Because…ow!" He'd grabbed the top of my ear this time, pinching it harder than he had my hand.

"I don't want to go in yet."

And he wouldn't let go, jabbing at me and hanging on harder each time. "Ow!" I'd yelled in pain over and over to no avail.

No empathy for pain he couldn't feel himself, Kiki had only laughed louder and louder in response each time I'd yelped.

He could not be blamed. And I wasn't able to pinch his foot or yank a wing to make him see this. The wild world he was bound for would volunteer to teach it to him though I didn't want it to.

Moving my hand with the bird on it further from my face, didn't this say as much? "You know, somebody's ready to be released."

Kiki jumped back onto the back of the chair unsteadily. "When?"

Hitting pay dirt, I'd drive this fact home so he would never forget it. That you don't bite humans. "Somebody is ready to be released. This is how you know. THIS IS HOW YOU KNOW."

"How?" He genuinely had no clue.

"They attack their mothers!" Heartbroken I'd said something this cruel, I thought I'd make light of it. That I'd laugh and pretend everything was all right still. "Go figure." Looking down onto my soiled leg, my fingers and ear all bitten up and still stinging with pain, I'd thrown in the towel. "I got to go in."

"Can I stay here?"

"Okay." I turned, almost scared to face him this time. My helpless baby bird who'd I'd adored gone in one afternoon of play attacking. "You all right?" An unsure hand held his way, I so hoped he wouldn't attack it this time. My heart, already ravaged by his having grown up in one fell swoop. "I'll see you later then?"

He'd gotten onto my hand without incident. "Don't go."

But I had to get away for a few moments of alone time. "I'll see you later then, okay?"

He'd taken wing, flying over to his tree branches. "Bring more worms?"

"All right." I'd made my mind up to leave. "Bye Kik."

But I didn't want to go. My eyes on him—over on his tree branch—he'd looked like the small, helpless bird I'd always known. I didn't want to go at all. Not really. Not without Kiki.

He might overheat out here in the rising sun. Or a raccoon might chew through the screen to corner him. Or a coyote could dig under to get inside. Or a hawk could tear through the flimsy top. Knowing all this, knowing he was no match for real wild animals, I leaned my forehead to his. And nuzzled him.

"Bye, Kik. He's my Kik. He's my Kik. OW!"

Lost in baby talk, I'd felt a stabbing pain in my forehead. The sharpened end of a beak having rammed through my bangs, I was sure Kiki had no intention of hurting me. Or had he? If I'd been small as a worm—would he have wolfed me down whole?

My fingers feeling for blood there, there wasn't any. Kiki had then jumped bodily onto my head. Teensy razor sharp talons piercing through to my hair, he truly was unable to do much damage there. Still, I'd screamed bloody murder. But this time only in fun to make him laugh.

"Ah! I'm attacked! It's The Birds! It's The Birds! Ahhhhh! Oh my God! It's Alfred Hitchcock's—the movie."

Reaching for Kiki, trying to get control of him, he'd gotten back onto my hand. But he'd pierced my skin there with his beak. Hurting like crazy, I'd held him before my face. His beak staying precariously open, I was almost honestly scared for real. But laughing, being attacked by something that I outweigh by a million pounds, I'd gotten some perspective finally.

I'd joked on. "OW! OW! I'm going to have nightmares tonight. I'm going to have nightmares."

As Kiki went back to his perch, flying from one hand to the other to get there, he knew I was relieved he'd gone. Trying to catch my breath, it didn't come easy. But I'd felt in the clear. And had calmed down because he had.

"Okay. Okay. All right. That was some fun." I looked myself over, a mess by now, bloodied and pooped on. "Some—I'm really…" In need of peace and a shower? "OUCH!"

Kiki had jumped playfully back onto my head again. "Scream some more!" Sharp nails pounding over my skull, his beak pulling my hair, he'd lost himself in the moment.

And I'd felt another little gift slide hot down my temple.

My laugh completely gone, Kiki hit me with a final, hard peck.

"Ow!" My fingers surveying the damage, I couldn't believe it. "Uh oh. Did he—is this what I think it is?" Pulling the present from my hair, I'm really feeling soiled now. "No—OH! Oh no."

Kiki having taken refuge up on my ponytail, looked down at me. "I didn't mean it!"

Knowing he was in trouble now, once again Mom laughed to slake his worries. Reaching up to help him down, he'd taught me a lot. "I feel like a statue—OW!" My finger caught in the pincer of his beak, this was painful. "Ow. In a park somewhere."

The bird standing on my hand, he'd looked into my face. "Am I in trouble again?" Worried he was, he'd raced back up my arm and hid at the back of the chair.

Fed up, I let him have it. "This is not the way you treat your mother." As I started to pretend cry to rub it in, it was only to teach the bird the error of his ways.

Sure enough, Kiki was back on my shoulder, worried for real. "I'm sorry. I'm sorry." Nervously pecking at my shirt, the lesson had sunk in!

"Ow. Ow." But I couldn't contain the joy I'd felt, just having him there, all full of remorse. And when I'd chortled stupidly again, he felt forgiven.

"I love you."

But he had a heck of a way of showing it—biting my at my earlobe again. Trying to peck free my shiny, diamond stud earring. "Okay. Owie. Ow." Then I got concerned of losing the earrings in the grass. "Those are diamond. You can't have them."

"Why not? You gave me the bolt. The button. Peanuts." Pinching the top of my ear as hard as he could, he demanded this toy.

"Ow! Ouch!" He wouldn't stop. Then he let go and I'd guffawed till I was out of breath. "Okay. I get the picture." Going for the diamond stud again, I'd hung on to it for dear life. "You can't have that. OW. OW." He was attacking my fingers, there to stop him from getting the earring. But I was sure my earlobe was bleeding by now. That somebody who weighed scant ounces had turned me into Van Gough.

Perching innocently on my finger again, he couldn't stop the giggles. "Yell again. It's funny."

And I'd taught him nothing today. Teenagers.

"Kiki!" The bird hopping up my arm, I put a hand out to snag him before he hurt me again. I'd looked off to Jeff, safe behind his lens. "These are the perils of rehabbing wildlife."

"But you love me!" Kiki then went airborne again, flying over to his tree branch. "You love me!"

And I had. More than life itself. Looking fondly over at him, I saluted, ready to leave him here with Jeff. "Okay. So long."

Black feathers soaring at my head again, he was out to stop me, suddenly upset I'd really do it. "Don't go. Not yet."

"Okay. Okay. All right. I'm going to go and..." I'd looked over my grubby new self, the bird hanging onto my hair so I couldn't leave. "Does anybody here have a Kleenex?"

He flew from my head back to my hand again. "Stay!"

"Does anybody here have a Kleenex? I have to go take a shower." This said, Kiki had grabbed the skin of my finger and yanked at it. "Ow, ow, ow, ow." Ad infinitum. This teen had learned a new game today. That you could hurt Mom all you wanted.

And still be loved.

Kiki made his way to the back of the chair, worried again. "You won't throw me out, will you?"

Our having discussed this issue in the abstract, the time seemed nigh. "Kik is going to be released this Wednesday."

He'd leaned into me, apprehension creasing his thoughts. "Not Wednesday. It'll be hotter than today."

Oh, he was right. "No, maybe Friday. When the weather's a little cooler." But even Friday was too soon. Weeks from now, maybe. "And um, and I'm less bit up. And pooped on. So..." I salute again. "Till then."

But after I'd gone into the house and gotten cleaned up, I'm came right back out to him. Armed with a fresh slew of worms, I was out to set things right between us. Lo and behold, this time as I sat in my chair playing Worm And Go Seek, Kiki gingerly took the worms I'd dropped in the grass. Not once drawing blood, he'd played by the rules too.

Though I'd called him, "Kikums? Kik?" he didn't once come in once for the kill. And why all the sudden manners with Mom?

I had on welder's goggles—the big plastic kind that encased the eyes.

And Jeff's giant blue ear mufflers, used for power tools.

And a crucifix—in case Kiki turned into a vampire while I was gone.

Holding a worm down to him, I'd found peace at last. "Kik, come here." Having gotten onto my hand to get it, moving him towards my eyes, I was at last safe as he flew back down to the grass. Having taken the worm, he still hadn't come back.

"Kik?" Doing this over and over again, I had to exclaim with a big, victorious smile. "It worked. He can't get my ears."

"!!?#?" Kiki had done the unthinkable. He'd sworn at me.

"What?" Not one for a confrontation, I'd pretended I hadn't heard a thing he'd said. Lifting one blue cone off my ear, I'd acted like he'd said nothing. "I can't hear him." Then I'd looked back down at the bird. "What? Kik? I can't hear ya. Wha…?"

"I said I love you."

And he thought I'd buy this? "Oh, oh. Okay. All right. Okay, Kik. I LOVE YOU!"

Outwitting Kiki at the game of Worm And Go Seek, I'd hardly felt invincible. With his release date rearing its ugly head, I'd be left with nothing more than fond memories of having been bitten. And cheated against. And pooped on. I'd arrive one day at the Pearly Gates bearing all this in my heart because of one glaring fact.

Love is the only baggage you can take with you.

CHAPTER 15 (VIDEO 15)
KIKI PREPARES FOR RELEASE

August 1, late morning

I was unable to sleep the whole night through. Kiki's ever dreaded release date had arrived all too soon. Having to set the little bird free into the cruel world had taken its toll on me. I'd only met him for the first time only nine weeks, and one day, ago. Our time together wholly too short. Kiki was now only about ten weeks old. Tops.

But release him—I had to.

I'd wanted a full life for Kiki. He was too smart to be confined to the tiny prison of a cage for his entire life. He'd deserved more than that. He needed to meet up with other grackles. Fly south for the winter. Meet someone nice to marry someday.

Yes, I'd wanted him to find that one true love—like my doves had, obviously in love with each other. They'd fed each other. Groomed each other. And looked out for each other each and every waking second of the day.

I knew it was time to give Kiki his freedom. With each passing day, he'd gotten more assertive with me—his mother. Lately, he'd gotten bored with each new toy sooner than usual. Once favoring shiny things, today he wasn't even enamored with his big bolt. With tapping at his wind chimes to make them sing. With cracking his peanuts open.

Kiki had even grown bored with our Which Hand game.

159

A game whereby he'd have to guess which closed hand held the peanut inside. Touching it with his beak, he had rarely ever been wrong. He'd been getting more nippy than usual too. Not knowing that he'd damaged my skin with his beak, or gave me pain, I was getting pretty well chewed up when trying to move him. Clean his cage. Catch him in the house. And it wasn't his fault. He needed the outside world now.

Not his adoptive mother.

Soon to be an empty nester, both of us stood outside in the picnic enclosure. Shrinking from the moment I would have to open that screen's zipper to let my Kiki go forever—how would I say goodbye to him? How would I relate to him what he'd meant to me?

How could I be assured he'd be out of harm's way when he'd finally gone?

Kiki had no way of knowing that today was THE day. That this was a game we'd only get to play once. And that was the part that had sickened me the most. Kiki had become the best part of my life. The best part of me.

Having to let the bird go in just a few short moments, having to say that final goodbye, what would be left of my ravaged heart? To say I was a coward would be an understatement. I knew what saying goodbye to my baby bird would feel like. It would feel like death.

Jeff had been right about all this back on May 29th. Right about not wanting me to take in the nestling bird. But while he'd only been trying to spare my feelings—it had been an honor to bring Kiki this far.

To the inevitable goodbye.

My feelings meant nothing compared to him having life. I'd been a mere mortal entrusted with a job given to me by The Lord. And so, I'd get this job done.

Trying to remain upbeat for Kiki's sake, I'd kept up a cheerful façade all morning. About to break the news to him of his release, he must remain happy at all costs. And he would remain happy—if I didn't ruin it for him. Ruin his one shot at happiness by being all glum about it.

Freedom.

The day unbearably hot outside, I'd set out more than one aluminum pie dish of water in the grass today for Kiki to cool off in. I'd stood watching in glee as the bird dunked his beak under the water over and over again. Coming up only to shake out his wings, he'd go right back under again. Kiki overjoyed by the simple experience of a bath, I'd been overjoyed too.

"Weeeee!" His joy was infectious.

So how would I say goodbye to the best part of my life?

Watching Kiki like the proud mother that I was, that anvil loomed ever larger over my head. With each passing second becoming more and more precious than the one before—I couldn't stand the thought. That it was all about to end. I had so much to be happy about. How Kiki had grown. How I'd gotten him here. To this point. To the very day I'd watch him leave me.

Today being that day, he'd fly away for good.

And I'd let him. Be happy for him. Try to go on living myself.

Positive that the news of his release today would thrill him, I was barely able to speak. Let alone tell Kiki what was soon to come. So I sort of put it off as long as possible.

"Kik, you like to take a bath?" My voice sounding foreign to me, I'd hoped he didn't pick up on it. It sounded constricted. Little. Frightened.

"See, I'm an eagle. Eagles love water, right?" He was so proud of how he'd overcome his fear of pie tins.

I'd laughed softly, my heart not in it. But I'd stay on the subject at hand, my heart afraid to move into the truth of what I was witnessing here. Which was the last bath I'd ever watch my beloved Kiki take in captivity. The world full of predators, it could very well be the last bath he'd ever take. Any awful thing that could happen, just might.

"You like to take a bath, huh?"

The bird looked up at me and then scratched behind his ear with a foot. "It's the best bath ever."

Jeff being here softening the blow, I spoke to him about Kiki. "Yes. He likes to take a bath."

I'd repeated this again, having stood there watching Kiki with bated breath. Taking it all in, our last moments together. Committing each little movement to memory. Marveling at how they'd stamped themselves upon my heart with the hard weight of forever.

"You like to take a bath, Kik? Yes?"

He jumped up on the ledge of the tin and shook himself off like a little dog. "All done," Kiki said, water flying off in all directions like he'd soon fly away from me.

My ankles splashed with water, I'd praise him, never to get the chance again. "Good boy."

I stood back as Kiki jumped up into the air. Looking for a place to land, he'd chosen the back of the red, white and blue camp chair he liked so much. Shaking his wings vigorously, droplets of water flying out again, I knew he couldn't fly well when water logged.

I didn't know what to do to slake my terrorized heart.

But it helped to put a soundtrack of words behind Kiki's every least little move for Jeff's sake. "There. Now he's going to dry off."

Then I had to laugh at how Kiki managed to turn himself into a little sprinkler. Dots of water splashing into my face, I'd moved in close to his body anyway. Loving how funny this little bird could be, the task at hand proved unbearable.

"Are you my good baby?"

"Mom. Stop."

"You're all wet. You're all wet. Like a little dog."

"No. Like an eagle." This again—he shakes water directly into my eyes on purpose to make me laugh. "Would you just *believe* in me for once?"

Not about to hurt his feelings by saying that I would do no such thing, I giggle instead. Moving ever closer, I'd crouched down to his level. And a fine spray splashes my lips and my too warm cheeks. "You're all we like a little dog. Yes you are. And you're blue. You're blue." Hint. Hint. I'd touched my forehead to the wet feathers of his back as he'd tried to shake his tail dry.

"Blue?" He'd paced the chair's back. "But I'm black and white."

Poor Kiki. About to be released and still, he wouldn't give up his dream of being what he could never be. "I love you. I love you Kik. I love you."

"I love you too." Jumping onto my back, he seems to float there.

Little feet tap dancing on my back, this is the best feeling ever. One I hope to never forget. "I love you, Kik. Kiki? Kik?" Getting up to a standing position, I'd forced him off, now somewhere behind myself.

I'd then heard a little voice. "Over here! Over here!"

Turning, I find him on his favorite perch—still shaking out the water from his feathers. "I love my Kik. Whoa!" Laughing as water pommels my face harder yet, I move towards the little bird regardless. "I love you."

"Why do you keep saying that?"

163

I was so happy for him. "Today's the day you're going to be released, Kik."

He'd tried to pick his feathers dry. "When?" Raking his beak through his chest, his wings—he'd tried to look unconcerned.

"You're going to be released in a few minutes." The words breaking my heart, I'd turned to Jeff, all the terror rushing headlong in. "He's going to be released." And I could barely believe I'd do it.

Kiki took this news well. "I'll look good. Meeting other birds for the first time."

"I know." I find myself telling Jeff something again about Kiki's release. "He wanted to be clean for it. He wanted to be clean for his release so he'd look nice. All day. For all the birds he's gonna meet. Right?" My attention on Kiki, I watch him rake his feathers faster.

"I'll need to get dry though." That said, it seemed as though Kiki was trying to prolong the inevitable goodbye too.

"He wanted to look his best. So I think that's good."

And I do think it's good. How Kiki will forget me once he's gone. Soon to be glad he'd left me perhaps. I'd watched him work on himself. Getting prepared to fly away for good. Still fearing that moment secretly so as to not alarm him.

"He's such a good boy." I'd said this again too, so Kiki knows how much I love him.

And it did seem like Kiki was trying to prepare himself mentally too. "I won't forget you, Mom. Don't worry."

"Yeah? Okay. And then you're going to remember…" Flinging water drops my way in order to get me to lighten up, I'd laughed. "Everything we'd talked about. Right?"

"Right," Kiki said. He didn't seem to be paying much attention—concerned more with drying his wings. Or maybe he was just trying to hide his fear from me.

Just as I'd been trying to hide mine from him.

I'd pressed on like a real trooper. "You're going to remember everything we talked about?"

Shaking out his body, his tail feathers, he'd whipped around suddenly. "I remember. But you can tell Jeff."

I freaked. The bird didn't remember what we'd discussed at all. Not the predators. Nothing. Ever the baby, I'd have to refresh his memory in case he'd really forgotten everything.

But I pretended to tell Jeff so that Kiki would overhear. And remember my words. "He's not going to go near owls. Or hawks."

"Or eagles?" Kiki circled on the perch, nervously shaking out the water now. "Eagles wouldn't hurt another eagle." He might as well have forgotten everything I'd told him thus far.

I put it out of my mind, how the dumb eagles would've eaten him for desert. "He's going to stay away from windows."

Because this was even more of a possibility than his trying to befriend a flock of eagles. Hitting a window, Kiki would knock himself out at once. Many bird collisions ending with a broken neck—and a quick death. And if not that, they'd be down on the ground unconscious. Thereby becoming easy prey for passing cats or dogs.

I could always pray that a good human would pick up my knocked-out Kiki. Place him out of harm's way. Say, up on a window sill. Or in a thick bush. Or up on a flower box somewhere—like I always did for bird collisions. Giving them half a chance to recuperate in peace, they usually woke up and flew away. And if they'd come down circling, a wing broken, they could always be brought into a wildlife center.

I'd moved on for Kiki's behalf. "And he's not going to land on people's heads." Which had become a bad habit of his. And he knew it had himself.

"I said I wouldn't."

"Is that right?" I'd chuckled. But shouldn't have, this being a really bad habit. People had no idea how helpless little birds are. Swatting them to the ground as if the bird could kill them.

Picking out his chest feathers with his beak, Kiki hadn't answered me. Ignoring my worries, really.

"Oh, and he's gonna find…"

"What? What will I find?"

"Worms?" I'd added, knowing Kiki really loved chewy bugs. "And he's gonna…"

"Eat them."

I move my face closer to his body. And I'd made him promise to do so—so he won't leave here and starve to death. "Yeah?"

"I like those big crunchy green and beige things."

"Oh, yeah?"

My own memory having lapsed, I recall that he had indeed liked those big crunchy things too. And I feel a little better, knowing he'd seek them out. Having an explosion of these insects this year, they hid underneath grape vine leafs. High up in the birch trees. The wild cherries. They seemed to be everywhere.

Bugs—manna from heaven for my Kiki.

And so I start to stupidly explain things again for Jeff's sake. "He likes those flying green things. We don't really know what they are. They're green." And I feel so dumb not be able to identify these insects, having an Audubon insect book too. "That's all we know. And…"

Kiki interrupts again. "I can fly that far. Up where they live."

"Okay. He's gonna, he's wants, he's been planning for a very long time…" I'm stuttering, worried his flying chops aren't quite up to snuff yet. And all because this very screened in tent was too small. "To, to go up in the trees." The trees seeming so big by comparison to him, my knees started to quiver in fright.

"The cherry trees." Kiki tried to extinguish my worry. "The green bugs are there."

So he knew this too. Somehow. His instincts being a complete wonder.

"Yeah. Okay."

Then again, the Japanese beetles being in the cherry trees had brought a fresh worry all their own. The trees being about four stories tall each, some branches were dead up there. What if a hawk saw him? A passing eagle? What if a raccoon was sleeping up there? What if Kiki injured a wing and couldn't get down? But I wouldn't let it show, these concerns. I just wouldn't.

I'd only spoken to Jeff instead, hiding it all. "He's had his eye on the cherry tree. There's a lot of cherries. And a lot of birds. In that tree. What else?"

I'd asked Kiki, pressing him for further proof that he's ready to find food on his own. He'd preened on, not knowing how vastly important all this was to me. News if he knew what else to eat, or not. But Kiki had only misunderstood what I'd asked with the words *what else*.

"I'm going to travel. See the world," he'd said, sure as any full sized eagle might be.

Pretending to be tickled by his plans, I hid my fear by laughing. But I was so scared of him being away from home, I'd started to get a headache.

"Okay. Okay," I'd babbled.

"I'll have such fun."

Kiki seemed excited, splashing water at me. He then turned around to face me so he could see me laugh again. Perhaps to have his own memories to whet one day when all the world stood between us.

And I'm talking to Jeff again. "He has plans to…"

Plans. Kiki seemed even more nervous at the thought. He'd never had to have plans before. So he'd jumped onto a perch. Then onto my hand. Then onto my shoulder. Then he flew back to his branch.

"Kiki has plans to fly south," I'd said, refreshing his memory of the *instincts* that should already be in existence there. "What are you going to do?" I'd leaned over to him just to be close.

And the seconds pulled us ever forward to the predestined path all humans and wild animals must take.

I'd pressed onwards. "To Tennessee. Or somewhere nice like that in the winter. Right?"

Hearing the question, Kiki had flown back up to my shoulder. "I'll miss you. I will."

"We talked about that."

Reaching up for the bird who'd soon leave me, I'd recalled getting the big atlas of the United States out of the car for him to see.

"We looked at flight plans," I'd said with a heavy heart.

Kiki having jumped up onto my other shoulder, I tried again to get him where I could see his beautiful face. Time of the essence, he'd stayed there where I couldn't get a clear view. But I'd smiled.

And all so I'd slake the anxiety. I didn't want to, in the distant future, mistakenly treat this day as if it had been any other.

I'd thought about my finger moving down the map for Kiki to watch. "We thought that maybe going down, straight down the Mississippi would, would be perfect."

Kiki jumped onto the top of my head as if just now getting cold feet about actually leaving.

But I couldn't let that happen. "Right?" I giggle so he'd think everything was all right. "Straight down the Mississippi. We thought that would be, um..."

I'd felt him dive off my hair for his perch. "The river looked long."

"That would be the best route."

I'd leaned my face into Kiki's as he sat in the sun. And yet, I was still worried he wasn't getting dry enough for flying.

But instead, hemmed in by the hellish heat, I'd found a cool resolve. "And, and so today we're going to, we're going to do it." Be set free. "But maybe we should wait till we're a little drier? So you can get some good altitude?"

My biggest fear was now that I'd set him free only to crash somewhere where a cat could get him. Many farm cats in the area, loose and roaming free themselves, were not fed. Many having believed they should kill things for their meals—mousers were born.

Birders.

Kiki seems to have picked up on this, splaying out his tail feathers. "I can't fly yet—wet like this."

Now I'd done it. Gone and wrecked his big moment for him. "You don't want to?" I ask stupidly.

He knew I wanted him to go. "I'm dry." He'd even checked beneath his wing as if to assure me that he was.

169

"Kik, but I think you should." Be completely dry before flying. "Altitude. It's all about altitude. You really need to get up in the trees. You're going to have to be dry, okay?"

"I'm dry. Look." He neared and allowed me to blow air over his body, out to help him dry. He seemed relieved. "That'll work."

Blowing air over him ever harder, I so hoped it would too. "That help? Did it help? Are you ready to be released?"

"Yes, Mom."

"Huh?" Our moment arriving all too soon, I'm devastated. But I wouldn't let him know it. I just wouldn't. "It's a great day. And…come here honey. Come here."

Having flown off his perch, when I'd pointed back for him to join me, he came back. "A great day, Mom."

Running out of time, things needed to be said. The proper thanks needed to be given.

"I thank the Lord, Jesus, for giving you to me. For such a short time." I'd choked up unreasonably, nearly able to go on. "And enriching my life." Fighting to keep the tears at bay, I'd bucked up, the smile a faltering one. "I swore I wouldn't cry."

Repeating this like a mantra, mantras don't work.

Kiki stopped preening, turned to me and locked his gaze with mine. "Why would you cry?"

He could be so innocent, this dear little bird. And that question proved he wouldn't know what death was until it came calling for him

I'd managed somehow to talk to Jeff again about Kiki. "He's happy. So I'm happy. Right?" And then all my love is right back with the tiny bird I'm about to lose forever. "I love you." Saying it again to Kiki, this time it had been said with a thorn stricken failing laugh.

Kiki stood stock still, as if chilled by the sound of it. "I can't leave if I can't fly. And I can't fly wet. I'll stay here then, Mom. With you."

I knew what Kiki was doing. He was changing his plans for my sake. Changing them back for him, I wouldn't think of keeping him in jail any longer. "I love you."

He would look me in the face. Wouldn't say a thing to me. "Kiki?"

"I won't go." His words were resolute. His feet, hanging tightly onto the branch with renewed strength. "I won't leave you. I won't."

It had been my turn to turn away. "I know. I know." I couldn't keep my voice from cracking, hard as I try. "You love me too." Noticing that he'd looked away, I saw that a bird had captured his attention. And I run with this. "But it's a big world out there. Look at that bird over there, man. He's free! And you're going to be free with him. And it's...oh!"

Kiki had gotten so excited, he'd had an accident. "I'm sorry."

I wasn't sorry. Knowing he was preparing to leave, to follow that other bird, I tried to help this along. "Lighten the load." And when I tittered to show him that it would be all right to leave this picnic tent, he still wouldn't. Instead, having flown back onto my shoulder.

"I won't go, Mom. I won't." Flying off me, circling, he'd only fluttered back to me again.

I had to somehow make my dearest little bird see that this would the right thing to do—to leave me. "And we're going to have a good time today. Are you ready to go?"

Sitting on my shoulder, all choked up, Kiki won't answer me.

Reaching back for his weightless body, him suddenly on my hand, he'd looked me squarely in the face. I'd asked him again. "Are you ready to go? Do you think you could?"

Having flown back to his perch, the sun on his back, his mind was made up. And I'd thought to find him an *out*. By doing so, I'd buy us some time to work out the logistics of this fatal parting.

Leaning down to him, I search his face. "Or are you too wet still?"

Kiki, shimmying off the last of the water, flew right back up onto my back. Out of reach again. And he was crying.

I couldn't allow him to go just yet. No. He couldn't go like this, all broken up. Confused. "I think you're too wet still."

"Mom, really." An unsure breath hovered at my ear as he'd somehow stopped shaking for my sake. "It's all right. I'm fine."

He was lying. Kiki was lying. And for my sake no less. He wasn't fine. Not fine at all. Getting him back onto my hand, I knew he hadn't been all right with this sudden departure. He wasn't ready to leave his mother just yet. No shame in that.

"Kik, I think you're too wet."

And this, I'd meant. He had to be in perfect flying shape his first time out. Perhaps even having to outfly the huge sharp shinned hawk I'd seen hanging around. Or the eagles I'd seen nesting in the dead trees near the huge pond at the other edge of the woods. The pond I would therefore never tell Kiki about—knowing that this would most likely be the first place he'd fly off to. The little fledgling—out to befriend something with real talons. Real sharp beaks.

Out to befriend eagles—that's what Kiki would do.

Lord help me. I didn't want this fledgy to ever actually leave me. And yet, I had to let him go.

Regardless, I'd tried to buy myself more time. "We have to wait a while, huh?" I'd hoped Kiki hadn't picked up on this change of heart.

But he had, saying what was on his mind. "You're scared I'll befriend the eagles. Then I won't go. I won't. How could I ever leave you anyway?" Jumping up onto my shoulder, his back to the world, he seemed ashamed of his words. His tears.

I could manage to say only one thing. "I love you."

"Mom!" He'd flown back up onto my head. I'd felt small talons jump off only to hang onto my pony tail for dear life. "No!"

"I love you, Kik!"

Leaving home would never be easy for anyone. And it certainly wasn't about to be easy for Kiki. A homeless. Motherless. Abandoned little blackbird. One who couldn't leave me this fine day anymore than I could leave him. Ever. And so, we'd had a problem here. Kiki and I.

Two inseparable beings—beings as different as night and day— would now have to find a way to say goodbye. Each of us, having to find a way to live successfully through the loss of their best friend.

Their reason for living.

CHAPTER 16 (VIDEO 16)
THE LONGEST GOODBYE

August 1, afternoon

We sat outside together in silence, enjoying our last moments together—Kiki and I. He sat on the back of my camp chair. I'd sat in it. Both of us, still locked safely inside the tent with the screened in sides, at least had this.

These few precious moments to just be together. Like always.

Waiting for Kiki's feathers to dry out, we'd been enjoying each other's company. Enjoying it for the last time perhaps. And these cherished moments had been going by way too fast. More than possible that this could be goodbye for forever—there was no going back now.

Thoughts rampaged mercilessly through my head. I went over things again and again, all that could go wrong. Released from here, Kiki may fly off—and keep flying until he became lost. Or he may get injured somewhere *out there* and never come back to me. It would be the *not knowing* that would be the painful part.

Not knowing if he'd lived the next few hours. Not knowing if he could really find food on his own. Not knowing if he'd come back for water. Not know if he'd been successfully released. Or not. After these next few moments together, it could be all over. All over.

The heat of the day rising, Kiki had flown down from the chair to get a sip of water. Coming right back up to sit on my outstretched hand proved I wasn't the only one worrying too.

"Hi, honey. Kik, I would like you to do me one favor."

Still sitting there, on my hand, he'd looked up into my face. "A favor?"

I don't know what else to say so I'd said this again. "I would like you to do me one favor."

"Anything." The bird nervously jumped onto my shoulder. Then on the back of the chair. Then onto my shoulder again. And there he'd waited raptly for an explanation.

"When I release you, Kik."

Kiki twirled my hair in his beak, fidgeting there. "I already know what you're about to say. Just, don't say it."

I had to smile, Kiki tickling my ear. But this bit of information, he had to hear. "I want you to remember that you're a grackle. Not an eagle. Can you do that for me?"

"How?" His back turned on me, he'd moved right back onto the chair's ledge again. Putting much needed space between us and the truth, he'd have none of either. "How, when I am an eagle?"

I'd try harder. I couldn't let him fly off and attempt innocent contact with a predator. "Kik? Can you do that for me, honey?"

"I won't. I can't. I'm an eagle, Mom. And when you least expect, I'll prove it to you." He'd moved from the chair back and went down to the arm of it. Then he came back to stand on my hand.

Holding firm on the issue, truth of the utmost importance, I wouldn't let him get away with this. Not when we've come this far together. The very end nearing.

"Can you remember you're a grackle? And not an eagle?" Holding a worm graciously out to him to eat, I don't think he'll take it from me. This peace offering.

But Kiki had taken the worm. Talking with his beak full, the small word is garbled. "You'll see."

I'd pushed on somehow by sheer force of will. Kiki could not leave here thinking he was an eagle. He just couldn't. The danger of this delusion insurmountable. "Huh? Can you remember that? I would like for you to remember that one thing."

"Why should I?" He'd flown back to the chair at my back, miffed. "Who says I can't be an eagle? Who?"

Unable to tell him the truth, that these giant birds—these eagles—would sooner kill him to eat than befriend him. But I wouldn't say it. I couldn't say it. "You're a grackle. Not an eagle."

"But why? Why can't I just be what I am?"

My heart breaking for Kiki, a bird with no real mentors, save for one hapless one, I lift a hand up to him and hope he'll rejoin me. "This way, you can, you can find a nice girl. I want you to fi…"

He'd touched my thumb lightly. My fingers. "You mean, a hen?" Having just argued semantics, he'd flown away from me. As if testing his feathers, it didn't seem he wanted to admit just yet that they'd dried.

I'd use his words then. "Yeah. A hen." And I'd meant a tiny little grackle hen. Not some big, fancy eagle lady with a white head and tail.

Kiki came back to me, sitting then on the arm of my chair. "Go on. I'm listening."

"A nice girl, okay?" I was thrilled when he'd climbed back aboard my hand again. "You find a nice girlfriend for yourself."

"Henfriend." Somewhat embarrassed that I'd drove home this point, Kiki dove behind me again, as if caught kissing some girl by his mother.

"And you—you're going to have a wonderful, long life." I'd leaned back to him.

"A life, yes." That said, Kiki nuzzled my fingers again as if making peace. "I know. I know. But without you."

"Right?" My very being demanded that I make him agree to this. "You're going to have a wonderful long life." It's what I'd prayed for mostly for him.

The small grackle seemed to stand a little bit taller. "And many nestlings of my own?"

"Yeah. That too. That too. Okay?" The thought of a wife and family finally electrifying him, he'd tested his wings again. Then he'd moved down to the grass to think about all this, the space between us oft putting.

I'd tapped the arm of the chair to get his attention. "Come here, sweetheart. Come here."

Kiki didn't trust this. "Is it time to go? I'm scared." The bird had stood his ground, immovable with fright, next to my feet.

"Come here, honey. Okay."

Leaning over, getting my beloved Kiki back up onto my finger, I'd held him up before my face. Then, mustering every ounce of courage I could summon—the time had come to end this thing.

So Kiki could begin his new life.

Without me.

"All right. We're going to walk out of this screened-in Coleman picnic tent."

"Why are you doing this to me?" That said, Kiki was gone in a flash of bluish black iridescence.

Looking this way and that for him, I saw that he'd staked out a place on the ground behind my chair. "Kik, you want to be released, don't you? Kik?"

Calling him like old times, this wasn't like old times at all. This was about broken hearts. And forever goodbyes. And the thought that maybe, just maybe, I'd never see him again. Not even in heaven.

"Kikums? Kiki?"

"Mom?" Moving out from beneath my chair, he'd obviously been thinking all the same things. "Mom?"

"Hi. Hi. Come on, sweetheart. Come on." But he doesn't come on at all, Kiki. And soon, I'm up and out of my chair in pursuit of him.

"I'll stay here. In the shade." And his mind's made up.

"We're going to be released, Kik." My hand held down to him, I wait there. "We're going to be released. Yeah. Come out of the dark."

Kiki flew up onto the chair arm and paced there. Staring at the zipper in the screen's wall, his eyes were filled with terror. "I don't know about this." Finally flying back over to the branch against the screened wall, he'd perched there.

I'd looked at him there, my one and only baby. My Kiki. The only thing standing between freedom and captivity—being one thin screen. Blinded by heartbreak, my knees shaking, I gathered a much needed bravery. And all at once, I'd put my own heart aside.

For the sake of his.

"I'm going to open this screen. And we're going to be released."

"Out there?" The bird staring out the screened wall, he'd stood only inches from the zipper I was about to slide open. "With the other birds?" Suddenly, he was no longer sure he'd like them, these winged strangers.

"Yes. With the other birds. You ready?"

The news bearing down hard on him, Kiki opened his beak. "Eagles look more threatening with their beaks open."

Too late for this conversation, he'd needed another gentle reminding of what he was. What he'd become. "You're such a good grackle. All right?"

He wouldn't hear of such things now. A terrified flapping of wings, he'd flown away from the closed zipper that led to impossible freedom.

"You're a grackle. Tell yourself…" I'd stopped, meeting up with him as he'd stood on the back of the chair again. "Keep telling yourself you're a grackle."

And if I hurt him at this point, he'd have to be hurt. I'd do anything to find him a life outside this horrible screen.

Kiki's feet hung tightly onto the back of the red, white and blue chair. "Eagles love flags. I love flags. I'm an eagle." He'd flown away again as if he didn't want to be hurt if I'd suggested otherwise. Landing on the grass again, he'd stood his ground there.

"I know you're patriotic. Okay?" Moving my feet slowly across the ground, Kiki having followed them, I slide towards the screened doorway. "You ready? Come on. We're going to walk right out of here."

But we weren't walking anywhere. Because Kiki had stopped at the base of his beloved flag chair. "But my chair!"

He'd wanted to bring his chair with him, wherever he was going.

"Come on, sweetheart."

Standing back, giving him room, he eventually flew to the base of the doorway by accident. Grasping him in my hand, I very awkwardly raised that dreaded zipper. Holding him to my heart for the last time, I was so happy for him. And sad for myself.

"Okay, Kik."

Then I'm talking to nobody, and everybody, all at once. If I say out loud this inconceivable thing, if I commit this action to the world, I might not lose my nerve doing it. And so I'd gone on to try.

But with every ounce of courage destroying me. "Kiki's ready. We're going to walk out of the Coleman picnic tent. And he's going to be released."

Raising the clutched bird to my ear, the doorway all at once open at our sides, he'd whispered one last thing to me.

"I love you. Mom."

Holding him in both my hands for the last time, I held him away from my face so I could look into his eyes. "Right, Kik. I love you. Remember, I..."

"I can't go." Not even squirming in my hands, his words still came panicked. "I love you. And you love me."

"I know. I know you love me too." The heat rising in my face, I'd fought off the tears with a weak chuckle. "We're supposed to be happy here. We're supposed to be happy. We are." Holding Kiki to my forehead, I didn't want him to see the falling tears. "I love you." I'd then looked into his eyes. "I love you, Kik."

But he'd only looked away. "Then why do I have to leave?"

I wouldn't answer this question. The bird of my lifeblood was young. Too young to know one salient fact. That the only kind of life worth living was a life of freedom.

"Are you ready? Are you...he's ready. Okay." Squirming in my hands, I knew he'd fly right back into the tent. So I did the impossible.

I'd walked out that door with my reason for living clutched in my hands.

And suddenly, nothing stood between Kiki and freedom any longer.

About to open my hands, this was our final moment together as mother and son. Soon my baby would be gone forever. Gulping down the heartache, this was the last thing in the world I could do. Let Kiki go. But do, I must.

Still, I could not believe where life had just lead us. The cruelty of this act—for us both—seemed utterly palpable. Yet, here I was standing, with the bird clutched in my hands. Ready to let him go. I was about to do a thing that could only be done just once in a lifetime. Having been unbearably choked up, I could barely talk. Barely able to get out the words. The pep talk I was now going to give—to none other than Kiki. And myself.

"Here we go, Kik. We're outside the picnic tent. And Kik's going to have a long, wonderful, happy life. Right?"

Kissing Kiki, my heart crushed, this couldn't be the last time my lips would meet his feathers. It couldn't be. But it was. It would be the last time. Ever.

"Mom?" Kiki no longer struggled in my hands as I'd held his body to my forehead. "Have a happy life—away from you?"

I'd held him in a way that I could see his eyes. Then I rubbed his face against my forehead. But he would be happy without me. He would. "I know you are, honey." I tried to be strong, for the both of us. "Are you ready?"

"No." Kiki gave up to fate, refusing to struggle in my hands.

"Are you ready?" I backed up as if to give him room, this little bird grasped in my hands. "Come on. There you go."

Lifting him up to the sky—I did the unthinkable.

I let Kiki go.

The bird gone, my arms stay outstretched to the sky. Closing my eyes for the briefest of seconds, I watched Kiki make a small circle. Then—given the choice of freedom—he gave it up.

Landing right back on my head.

Fists clutched at my chin, I'd laughed at how he'd come back to me. Though relieved for this little reprieve, the bird needed a little reminder. It didn't matter that it would surely destroy me.

"Kik? Kik? You're free." Wiping the tears from my eyes, I could not believe this was happening. That the bird stayed close to me. Out here! Stayed right on top of my head. "Kik, you're free to go."

"I don't care." Staying put, small toes clutched at my hair. "I'm staying. With you."

"Kik? You're free to go—any time you want." I'd waited.

He wouldn't answer me, hiding there on top of my head.

"Kikums?"

"I want to stay here. With you."

Laughing my heart out that a wild bird chose me over abrupt independence, I was shaken to the core. "Kiki? Kik? Ki—Kik?" Laughing through the tears that were still falling, the nervous laugh held me in the palm of its hand. "Kik? You're free!"

"I don't care."

"Kik?" My nerves shot, this just hadn't been working. At all. And I gave in to that. "Okay. Maybe not. We're free to go. But we're not going. Okay." I'd dabbed my wrist at my eyes, sure my black mascara wasn't holding. Sure dark blotches were flowing down my cheeks.

Then Kiki had mumbled something.

"What?"

He'd hung on for dear life, still on my head. "You're crying. You don't really want me to go. And I love you."

"I know. I know. I know you love Mom."

"But...?"

"What?" I'd asked.

The bird trembled there. "I thought you loved me. Like I love you."

My heart unable to take anymore, the words left me. "Okay. I know."

"Please don't make me leave home. I love it here. With you."

My voice had become a mere whisper. "I know." Holding a fist to my forehead, I could no longer keep it together for his sake. "I know, Kik. I feel the same way."

"I'm staying." He nervously pecked at my ponytail.

I felt small strands of hair being tugged. "Kik? Come on, honey." I laughed to make light of his going again. I'd lifted a hand up for him to stand on if he'd wanted to.

Climbing on, he held on with all his might. "Just a few more minutes then?" The wide sky all around us, nothing standing between him and liberty, he'd hung on tightly to the only home he'd ever known.

Me.

"You're free. You're free, sweetheart. You need to leave now."

"No." He stayed there, on my hand, his little legs trembling.

"Okay. Look it." I had no idea what to say to him to make him see that he should choose freedom.

I looked around at the big wide world, blooming massively at his tiny black back. Looked at the endless expanse of sky. At the tall, shady trees that should beacon him away from me. And it seemed incredulous—that Kiki was still here. On my hand.

And so I'd told him as much. "We're not in the tent anymore. We're not in, inside the screen."

He surveyed the yard he'd so longed to be free in. "It doesn't matter. It's pretty. But I've made my choice."

"I know, it's wha…?" I'd wait for him to finish the sentence.

He'd looked around as if seeing the world for the first time. "Beautiful."

Bingo. "It's beautiful." I was sure we'd hit a turning point here. "Right. And there's the hummingbirds."

He'd looked off to where I'd wanted him to. "Yes. I see them. Over there."

"Isn't it pretty?"

"But Mom. I love you."

"I love you." Going to kiss him again, this time he'd moved away. Hurt and yet joyful he'd done it, I'd let him know how I still felt about him. "I love you."

"I can stay in the cage. Forever." His beak open, drying out, his own discomfort finally registered. "I'm thirsty."

"I know. You want to go by the water thing?" The bird bath. "You want to go by the water thing? There it is. There." Bending down to place his feet on its rim, he'd flown off, scared. Never having been this close to it before.

"I'm not ready. To be with them." The other birds.

Having flown to the low evergreen bush at my back, I turned to face him. Very proud he'd taken this little step towards independence, it was better than clinging to me. And yet, he couldn't very well stay there either. Out in the open. Easy prey for all the hawks in the area.

"There you go. You're free! You're free, honey."

"I am? I am?" Fluttering his wings, he'd turned to face me. And he'd stayed standing on the bush as I bent down to speak with him too.

"You're free. Yes you are. Yes you are."

He'd looked down at the grass at my feet. "You're there. And I'm here. And I'm still alive."

All true. Every word. "Okay?" I'd reached a finger out to him.

Flying this way and that, then facing me again, he'd held on with his toes. "It's different. Holding on. This time."

"You're free." Still crying, sniffling, I hadn't heard what he'd said. "What?"

"But love?"

I knew just how he'd felt. "I know. I know. You too?"

"Mom, I you know I love you." He turned away from me and looked up at the old locust tree towering over us. "There's so many perches up there."

"Yes." I looked up with him, seeing for the first time, through his eyes, how Kiki saw a tree. "It's a big world. It's a huge world. And you're in it now."

He eyed all the endless space. "It's all mine?"

Finally. Progress. "There's no more carriers. Or screened in porches. Or cages. Or anything. It's just you and this."

"I love you though."

"I love you." No sooner had I said this, I felt his feet clutch my hand harder—a loud car approaching.

"A car's coming."

"I know. A car, yeah. You stay away from cars."

Cars were loud. They were fast. And they were deadly to a bird. The thought occurred to me to grab Kiki and run for the house. But no. This had to be done. I had to destroy that place in my heart where Kiki resided so that he may live.

"You stay away from them." The cars.

"I will. I will," he'd promised.

I touched my forehead to Kiki's back, sure I would never lose him to a car accident. Sure he would stay away from the street. From anything speeding at him. And yet, what if he didn't?

"I love you, Kik," I'd whispered. Nuzzling him again, how could I do this, let him go? A car speeding past again, I so prayed one would never hit him. "I love you, sweetheart." I rubbed my tears against his wings so he'd wear them forever in remembrance of me. His mother. "I love you, honey."

He'd only looked up at the unending sky. "I can do it. I can do it. I'm an eagle."

My cheek against his wing, I'd moved away. If he needed to be an eagle to do this, to leave me, I would not say a thing against it. "Go on. Go in the tree. Go in that tree! Do it! Do it!"

"I will! I will!" But Kiki had stayed put, perched on that single index finger, his knees still shaking.

Unable to contain a laugh, I'd rubbed my tears away. Making him at least jump from one hand to the other, I'd hoped the movement would loosen up his grip of my finger. "Okay, you ready? You ready?"

Kiki turned his head around to peer into my face. "Do you mean it?" He'd then faced down the huge locust tree, its branches looming over his little birdy head.

"That tree." I did mean it. I did. And despite myself too. Pointing to the very tree in question, he must fly to it. "Aim for that tree. Go."

Pushing my hand upwards, Kiki had lifted off. Praying he'd be okay, my hands held together in the air, he'd landed right back on my head. Bursting into thankful laughter for this one blessed second more to spend together, I'd also whispered to myself. Whispered about the dismay I'd felt—that my heart would have to bear this longer than it had to.

"He's not going to leave." Getting out a hankie to wipe away the onslaught of tears, Kiki had hung onto my hair.

"I can't. You're crying."

A small plane flew overhead. Low to the ground, its engine roaring, I couldn't hear him. "What?"

"You're crying. And I'm scared too."

"I know. I know it's scary." Lifting him off my head with my hand, it didn't seem this would ever end. The longest goodbye in history, our hearts were both irreparably ripped up by it. My very words, shredded by the tears. "I know it's scary. You don't have to be scared."

"Mom?" He'd turned and stared into my eyes, eyes that didn't easily lie. His own eyes now brimming with tears. "That's the first time you ever lied to me."

I smiled at him. I shook my head no. And all to show that I wasn't frightened for him. But he knew me, Kiki. He knew me better than I knew myself.

But he had to believe what I was about to say. "You don't have to be scared, okay?" But he did. He did have to be scared. Knowing the reality of his going, he didn't know the half of it. Everything out here could potentially kill him. Just everything.

"Mom, if I go…" He looked back at the tree then silently faced me while I broke into a horrible crying jag. "Where will you be?"

"I'm right here." I could barely talk. "I'm right here. Kik? You, you're making this hard on me."

Kiki had bent over and kissed my thumb. "But I'm not." Then his tears grew right along with mine.

"You are," I admitted, barely able to say the words.

"I can't leave. I love you."

I rubbed at my eyes. "I know. But..."

"There's more, Mom."

"What else?"

Kiki had looked down at the ground. "What if I get lost? What if I never see you again. What if the world is an awful place?"

Stunned, the same doubts having occurred to him as well, I felt guilty for putting them in his head. "It won't be bad."

"Without you, it will be awful." That said, Kiki flew to my shoulder like old times.

I didn't know what to say. Rubbing my face against his, I'd turned, speaking ever so softly. "Kik? I love you."

"I'll need this." Out to make me laugh, he'd tugged at my earring.

And it worked. He'd stunned me into that old dumb giggle. "That's a diamond!" The same one he'd tried to steal when we'd played Worm And Go Seek back in our better days. A diamond soon to be plucked off and lost in the grass.

But Kiki had grown honestly insistent. "I need it to sell."

Feeling my earlobe, I'd made sure the stupid stone was still there. "No, no you can't have it to hock out on the free market." Or black market, I should've said.

But he'd grown resolute. And the more I tried to hang on to the earring, the more he'd tugged to get it loose. "I need money."

Poked with the tip of his beak accidently, it hurt. "Ow! Ow! Ow!" This again. "Ow!"

Kiki had mumbled something.

I got him back onto my hand, my mascara now melting down my cheek. "What?"

"I need the earring. Or I won't go."

I'd quickly figured out where he was going with this. "You don't need, you don't need diamonds."

"How will I pay for food?"

"You don't need anything . The bugs are out here. And…"

He turned to look back at the bird bath. "What is that thing?"

"It's a—there's water. And, remember? If you want to go to the rivers you can do that." We'd seen the Mississippi for ourselves once. On the atlas.

Kiki panted to show me his distress, the heat of the day ever rising. "I'm hot."

"I know you're hot." I'd rubbed at my nose, fraught with full blown sniffles as he shook out his feathers. "I know you're hot." I so hoped he wasn't overheating. How would I ever send him off with heat exhaustion? "Are you good? Are you good, sweetheart?" I looked up at the cool shade of the tree. So many leaves to hide behind. "You want to try for the big tree?"

"Yes." Bending over to kiss the tip of my index finger, this could be it.

This could be the very moment I lost Kiki forever.

And yet, I resolved to do just that. Despite my ever weakening resolve to say goodbye, I'd tried. "Okay. We'll try it again. We'll try it again." And I'd pushed Kiki off my hand once more.

The tall tree worrisome, the bird had flown right back into the low bush at my back. "I like it here."

"You like that?" The bush not an option due to his being too out in the open, I'd scooped Kiki right back up in my hands.

Alighting again, flying around me in a tiny circle, he'd landed right back on my shoulder again. "I can't do it. I can't fly away with a heavy heart."

I'd started to laugh so he'd feel better about leaving me, the only mother he'd ever know, and I'd reached out a hand to him again.

And just then, the mail truck had pulled up to the box. A red Jeep, though it had stayed out on the street, it had stopped menacingly at our side.

Kiki, not knowing why this car had stopped, suddenly flew away.

For good.

My laughter stopping all at once, I'd watching him go very high up. Circling over the roof of the house, I remained stunned to see the wide blue sky behind my tiny little bird. And I'd grew faint at the sight. My knees giving out, my legs buckled out from underneath me. I caught myself, stumbling around to do it.

And I could barely find the words, losing my beloved Kiki forever. And all at once. "He's, he's in the sky!" Looking down to thank the Lord, I'd looked back up quickly. Fearing I'd never see Kiki again, I then saw something magical.

Kiki had a white head. A white tail.

I glanced towards Jeff. "I could've swore, for one se—second. Or maybe the sun was in my eye. He was an EAGLE!" Never having been this happy in all my days, the laugh was breathtaking. "He was an eagle!" And soon I'd found myself yelling at the top of my lungs. "I love you, Kik! I LOVE YOU!" And then the prayers really started. "Thank you, Jesus." And the tears came back. "Thank you, Jesus. Please keep him safe. Please keep him safe and happy. Thank you. Thank you, Lord."

Breaking down, crying as hard as I'd ever cried in my life, it was over.

"Oh, God. I love you, Kik. Wherever you are."

Feeling very alone, my life had changed right along with his. In the instant of this small goodbye, Kiki had flown away with my heart. And I'd never be the same without him. And yet, having known him, I knew my life would be better—after my heart let him go too.

"Thank you, Jesus." I dried my tears and had to laugh. "This was the best day of my life."

I was so happy for Kiki, somewhere away from me now. And free. Free to be the bird he was meant to be. Though I'd shook my head, I knew I'd done the right thing by him. By this rare little gift entrusted to me. And I spoke to the Lord, to reassure him, rubbing at my arms.

"I'm good. I'm good."

And, holding my hanky to the very cheek that had touched Kiki's wing, it was as if I could still feel his feathers there. Warm against me. And I'd have this forever, this feeling that I'd touched one of God's creatures. Then, when the truth hit me all at once, I'd said as much.

"It's never easy when kids leave home." Laughing at my own lame joke for respite, the laughter was fleeting. "It's never easy." Sniffling, I bucked up and made my peace with what had just happened. "Okay. Okay."

Then, walking away, making my way down the driveway for the front door, this had been the hardest thing I'd ever done. In my life. Making my Kiki leave me. And watching him go. Being gone—just like that. And wasn't this just the cruelest thing of all? To find out what the heart was capable of doing when left at the mercy of itself?

Love, lost in the blink of an eye, only grows ever larger.

CHAPTER 17 (VIDEO 17)
GREATEST OF MIRACLES

August 12, late afternoon

The day after I'd released Kiki there'd been a terrible thunder storm. Hard rain. Heavy wind. Lightning. So many days I'd regretted setting him free. If only I'd waited a few days longer. In agony, I'd often wondered where he'd spent that night—a frightened little bird unused to being outside. I'd wondered where he could've possibly found shelter. There'd been no way he could have. And no way I could've shown him how to beforehand.

The weather being perfect on this day, I'd so wished I could've spent the day outside. With him.

But Kiki was still gone. I thought I would've seen him by now. Had thought that maybe he'd stay close to home. Close to me. Thought that he'd eventually show up in the yard one day to surprise me.

The days adding up brutally, I'd still had no sightings of him. Still hadn't heard that grackle *chuck-chuck* sound he'd made. Though I'd stood out in the yard waiting to hear it on countless occasions. Though I'd listened intently for it, the only time I'd heard Kiki's voice was when I was inside the house. In the basement. In my bedroom. The kitchen.

But this being a mere haunting of my heart, it was never real. Never.

After nearly two weeks passing since I last saw my Kiki, I was giving up hope of ever seeing him again. I wouldn't see him no matter how much I'd prayed for one more moment together. For one more second. For a chance sighting. Because none ever came. No matter how much time I'd spent looking out the windows, binoculars in hand.

My little Kiki hadn't showed up at the bird bath for water. He hadn't stopped by the feeders for seed. He hadn't picked around in the cherry trees for fruit. He hadn't fluttered down onto the grape vines. All his favorite green insects hiding there under their wide leaves. Though I'd seen countless other birds doing these very same things—not a single bird was ever him. I'd never see my Kiki again. I knew this by now, miscry gnawing away at me in my weakest moments.

I missed the way Kiki would look at me. As if I, the center of his universe, could do no wrong. I missed the way he always dunked all his food into his water dish before eating it. Missed the games he'd invented to make me laugh. Running precariously through my shoes on the rebounder. Or making me find my missing jewelry. Everything carefully hidden in his seed cup alongside other shiny stuff. Bolts. Metal washers. Pieces of tin foil.

Glad I'd had the foresight to save every single baby feather Kiki had ever shed, it only hurt to look at them now. All his beloved teething toys, abandoned and left behind too. Abandoned right along with me. To protect my heart, I'd taken down his cage. The wind chime, the one he'd loved to make ring, now sitting silent. The silver Christmas bell I'd hung from his cage to ring, now just a silent ornament again.

His baby perch, sitting alone on the fireplace mantel, had no little toes clinging to it anymore. Hard to look at, I should burn it. But I could no sooner do that than toss my own heart into a fire.

In the limitless depths of my caring, it just felt like something had gone wrong. So very, very wrong. With Kiki's growing absence, I knew that this could be the end of us. Something might have gotten him. Caught him. Ate him. A cat. A hawk. An owl.

An eagle.

I'd seen a raccoon recently catch a chipmunk while it came from its hole. And kill it. Kill it so swiftly and so unmercifully, the poor thing never even had the chance to squeak. The awful sight startling, it remained an unforgiving thought that wouldn't release me. That my baby could've ended up mere food for another animal.

Or, God forbid, he'd flown across the street. Tangled with the very cars I'd begged him to avoid.

Unable to endure much more of this self torture, I'd had enough. One way or another, I needed closure. Today was the day. Putting a couple of shelled walnut pieces in my pocket, I was *that* sure I'd find my baby. But, going outside to look for my lost Kiki, my nerves stayed on edge.

Jumping when the screen door slammed at my back, I set out to actually find him. Or die trying. Setting off on foot, I'd first canvassed the woods out back. Calling his name as I walked along the path, I listened for his voice. I'd chuck-chucked too, hoping he'd do the same in answer.

But that answer never came.

I soon gotten the notion that if Kiki had indeed still been here— alive—he'd have flown down to me. Landed on my head. On the ground before me. But, having made my way through the woods, I'd come out onto the street. A good half mile from home, I should've seen something by now. Shuffling up the hill in utter despair, paying no attention to anything, I was lucky a car or tractor didn't kill me.

Lost in thought, chance memories skittered by. Opening me up like a bloody wound, the world seemed oddly quiet for this time of morning. Then, looking far in the distance, I thought I saw something up ahead. In the road.

And it was not good.

Running towards the apparition out of breath, my heart sank to my knees. This bird, dead on the street before me, was black. All black. And it had been hit by a car a long time ago—this black bird. My heart racing out of control, I fell down to my knees on the roadway before it. Sharpened pea gravel digging into my skin, I'd barely felt the pain.

All I could hear was Kiki's last words to me. *I can't do it. I can't fly away with a heavy heart.* And what tiny eagle could— loaded down with such a big heart? Hadn't it been me who'd forced him into the fierce wilderness? Me? His own mother? This little songbird, the one who'd asked only for me to believe in him—had been here all along. Right here as if waiting for me to find him.

He'd tried to come home to me again. And this is what happened.

"Kiki?" My trembling fingers reached out to touch this dead thing I'd hardly recognized. But each had stopped there, inches away, before touching his spent body. "Kiki?" Not even enough bird left to bury, I would not cry having to leave him there. Not yet. Not here.

Having asked the Lord to take my Kiki to heaven, I'd said my prayers. I'd made my peace with this loss. Then I stood back up somehow.

And so this is why my beloved baby, my Kiki, had never come back home. To me.

Not above blaming myself for having let him go in the first place, I'd stumbled home. Still, I'd kept the tears at bay. I just wouldn't cry. Not yet.

Standing at the large expanse of windows in the living room, I'd looked out on what had been Kiki's world. The sky. The trees. The birds at the feeders. Cool air-conditioning pressing in all around me, I suddenly felt as though I was on fire. My temperature, my blood pressure, everything going up. With my forehead pressed up against the cool glass, I had to admit the truth to myself.

I was never to see my Kiki alive again.

Obvious to me by now, I'd opened the window and called his name anyway. I'd called him until my throat went hoarse. And all right, well, since Kiki hadn't answered me—that was him in the road.

Knowing he'd been given a mercifully quick death, I should be thankful. And I'd tried to be. But, as I'd turned away from the window, my life irrevocably changed, I thought I'd heard Kiki go *chuck-chuck*. Thought I'd heard that familiar sound he'd made so often when he was happy. And wasn't this just the final insult? Staring outside blankly, raw emotions flooding in, I could no longer keep the onslaught of tears at bay.

Kiki was so wonderful. So playful. So smart. To say I'd missed him would not only be an understatement, it would be laughably so. I'd missed Kiki not only with all my heart and all my soul, but with something unnamed that was bigger than each. If that were possible. The thought of never being able to see him again, to touch him, it had killed some part of me. Killed it as dead as the bird I'd chanced upon in the street.

And then the blame came.

How could I have let him go, my baby bird? How? Other people kept grackles as pets all the time. All the time. The world outside the window wavering with hard earned tears, I stood there for a very long time. Crying. Just crying. I stood there until I could cry no more. Till my eyes went dry. And though I'd somehow managed to stop, a painful lump lodged thereafter in my throat.

Then suddenly, I thought a black streak flew past the window.

A bird that flew into the tree line somewhere at the back of the house. And it had landed in the very area where a fledgling Kiki had stood on his curtain dreaming he'd one day be.

Running through the kitchen for the back door, shouting for Jeff to get his camera, we both stumbled down the back staircase. And there he was!

There stood my Kiki!

And he'd stood right on the stair railing that led down to the valley beyond.

"Mom?"

"Kiki?" Barely able to breath, I'd run down to where he stood waiting for me.

Approaching him with my hand out, I was scared he might have gone too wild to allow a human to approach. As an adult, he might think I'd be out to trap him—like he got trapped by humans when a baby. Fearing I'd scare him away, my heart swelling at the sight of him—I'd put out a hand anyway.

And Kiki jumped right into my hand like no time at all had passed by.

I barely knew what to say. Was worried the sound of my voice might drive him away. "Hi. Hello. Hi! Where have you been?"

"Hungry." Kiki hungrily gobbled up the small scattering of crushed walnut in my palm as if he'd never left.

"Where have you been? You've been gone eleven days."

"I got lost." Jumping back on the railing, he pointed to the woods with his beak. "Out there."

I didn't care why he was gone. The main thing being that he was home now. "Hi Kik. Kiki! Kik!" His name upon my lips, I felt alive again. I'd approached him, my hand out, full of food again. "Hi baby."

"Hi, Mom. "He's grabbed my finger with his foot and held on, touching it lightly as he ate.

Stupefied to be with Kiki again, I almost forgot how to talk. "Hi." No more than inches before my face, him being here was an answered prayer. A miracle. My little miracle. "You've been gone eleven days. Where were you?"

"Looking for chicks."

Stunned speechless that Kiki had found somebody, I'd gone from complete desolation to a dream coming to fruition in seconds. Left stammering like I'd been born brainless, Kiki kick started my head for me. He did so by flinging a piece of walnut at my lip, snapping me out of it. And when I'd spit that shard back into the air, I had at once gained my footing.

My eyes, having fallen over his beautifully iridescent adult self, of course he'd been looking for chicks. "You were?"

"Yeah."

My whole body felt all lit up with a smile. My Kik had found someone. Someone to love. "Then what?" He'd stepped onto the palm of my hand like old times. "Then what did you do, honey? Hi, I'm so glad you're…"

He'd mumbled something. His beak full, I couldn't understand him.

"What?"

He'd looked off into the distance for a moment. "That big storm? I tried to fly away from it. When I stopped, I was lost."

"That…" Now I'd really felt I'd let him down. Having released him before a storm front. "Oh." The guilt was hideous.

"Don't blame yourself. I shouldn't have said anything."

This time, I'd try to make a joke to slake his worries. "I….you could've called. I was worried." But I'd smiled to let him know I'd been joking. Careful to never instill guilt for his having left me.

It was his God given right—to live a bird's life.

"Mom, I love you."

I'd smiled. I'd laughed. My heart just sang, him here with me again. "I love you." Watching him fly off, I suddenly worried I'd never see him again. "I, here, oh." He'd only flown in a tight little circle in order to land on my wrist. "Hi."

"I could never leave you."

"I know. I love you, Kik." Holding my arm before my face, Kiki eating the nut held between my fingers, I could not believe my eyes. "I love you."

Kiki tugged at the walnut with the tweezers of his beak. "What have you been doing?"

Not being important, how I'd been crying, I was worried only for him. "What are you going to do, Kik? What are you going to do?"

My beloved bird jumped onto my upper arm. And then he'd looked out over the forest beyond. "I don't know yet." Then he was back upon my shoulder as if he'd never left.

"Here you go. There." I put the nut in my open palm and watched him eat it. A blessing—him being only inches from my eyes. "I love you." Leaning in to kiss him, he'd leaned towards my lips.

But he seemed stunned, catching himself. "What if the other birds see this?"

I'd giggled at how he'd cared about their opinion of him. "I love you. I do. I love you. Where have you been?" I'd really been interested in what he'd seen of the world.

"I found a pond." He'd whispered into my ear, the sounds of birds all around in the woods. Watching. Listening. "On the other side of the woods."

Our neighbor's pond. Spring fed. Stocked with fish. And eagles.

"What?" His having come back unscathed, I stood shocked. I'd so hoped he'd outwit predators. And this proved he had. "No. You're kidding? You're kidding? Then what?"

"I found crawdads there. And I met birds. Like myself."

Not knowing whether he'd meant grackles or eagles, I'd let the statement slide.

Just glad he'd come back, I'd remind him to come home a little sooner, the next time. "You stayed away from Mom for almost two weeks."

"It was hard." He'd picked at the tie I'd worn around my neck, his favorite cross dangling from it. "Finding my way back."

I'd repeat this so he'd know how he'd hurt me. "You stayed away from Mom for almost two weeks."

"But you cried when I left. Then you were just in the window—crying again."

"You saw me in the window?" I tell Jeff because he hadn't known this. "I was crying in the window." Having said this, having outlived the hurt, it was all such a wonder. And so I'd smiled.

"Bye." Kiki had inexplicably flown off behind me, something pressing to attend to.

Hearing the last of his beating wings, I knew he'd be back again.

"Where'd he go?" Turning in a circle, I hadn't seen which direction he'd flown off to. But this time, I didn't feel so lost without him. "Kikums?" I'd held up my palm, another nut in it, trying to lure him back. "Come here, honey. Kikums? Kikums. Kikums."

I'd looked around but my visitor was nowhere to be found. Not in the cherry trees. Not at the bird feeders. Not at the bird bath. Kiki seemed to be nowhere and yet everywhere—all at once. And because of that, because of his hidden nearness, my heart alighted. It nearly seemed to have flown away with his. And there my heart would stay. With Kiki's.

Wherever he'd gone off to.

"Kiki!" Then all at once it hit me like a falling anvil. "KIKI'S HOME!"

All the pain and heartache suddenly lifting with these words, I'd lifted my arms in the air. And jumped up and down like a complete idiot.

"Kiki's home! Kiki's home!"

Then I laid it all out the worst of it for myself, all that had happened, in mock anger. "He didn't come back to see Mom. He didn't call. Or anything. For almost two weeks." But it made me happy, how Kiki was watching the house all along. "I think he saw me in the window. I was—not good. Earlier." I jumped up and down again, happy for the first time in what felt like years. "I'm good now!" I'd turned to the woods to say it to Kiki. "I'm good now, Kiki! Kik!"

I couldn't contain the happiness.

"He'll come back. I'm, I'm, I have…" Lord, what did I have that Kiki liked so much? I was so full of joy, I had no idea. Oh right. "I have walnuts." And suddenly, the key to all my happiness was having walnuts to share with my dearest baby bird. "I have walnuts."

I saw a bird soar over.

"There he is!" But while the bird hadn't been Kiki at all, what it was seemed funny somehow. "No. That was a blue jay. A Kiki imposter."

Turning towards the forest at my back, he was out there somewhere. The real Kiki. The living Kiki. Now, at least, I had this knowledge. That even though I sometimes couldn't see him, that didn't mean he wasn't somewhere out there watching me.

"Kik? Kikums? Kiki?" Not hearing an answer, not hearing his *chuck-chuck*—it no longer mattered. What mattered was this.

Kiki was out there. And he always would be.

"I love you!" The thought overjoyed me. "I Love you."

Hearing no response this time, it didn't matter. My life was changed the second Kiki had arrived home.

And I said as much to Jeff. "It's a great day."

And I knew who to thank for a day such as this.

"Thank you, Lord. Thank you." I bit back the tears. Tears of joy this time around. "I'm happy. And yet, I've been crazy."

And I knew why. My gift. My little gift from God had returned. And I said it to this bird, wherever he may be.

"I love you, Kik."

I'd even made the chuck-chuck sound. Playfully daring him to come and land by me again. But when he didn't—it didn't matter.

He was *out there*. And I knew that he was even though I couldn't see him.

Arms wide open to the world, his world, I'd scream out the words for everybody to hear. "I love you, Kik!"

Spinning round and round, dancing like a fool, joy like this happens only once in a lifetime. For only once in a lifetime does a miracle like Kiki enter your heart. And wasn't this the greatest miracle of all? Kiki, my majestic full grown grackle, just let me know he'd found his freedom.

In the exact forest I'd promised him back when he was a baby perched on a curtain rod.

www.ingramcontent.com/pod-product-compliance
Lightning Source LLC
Chambersburg PA
CBHW030319290526
45785CB00001B/436